Birds, Art & Design

Birds, Art & Design

LARRY BARTH

STACKPOLE
BOOKS

Published by
STACKPOLE BOOKS
5067 Ritter Road
Mechanicsburg, PA 17055
www.stackpolebooks.com

Printed in the United States of America

10 9 8 7 6 5 4 3 2 1

First edition

Photos of *Winter Lakeshore, Terns in Flight, The Wood Warblers, Vantage Point,
    In the Cattails, Great Reed Warbler, Green Heron, Tidal Companions,
    Broad-winged Hawk, Winter Sanderlings, Red-billed Tropicbird,* and
    Curves and Angles by Bill Einsig
Photos of *Killdeer, Marsh Hawk, End of Autumn, Winter Bohemians,
    Algonquin, Loyalhanna,* and *Solitude* by Alan Wycheck
Photos of *Bering Sea Pirates* and *Winter Waxwings* by Peter Vance
Photos of *In the Hemlocks* by Jordan de Guzman
Photos of *Wind River Harmony* by Phillip Harsh
Unless otherwise credited, photos are courtesy of the author

Library of Congress Cataloging-in-Publication Data

Barth, Larry, 1957– author.
  Birds, art & design / Larry Barth. — First edition.
      pages cm
   ISBN 978-0-8117-1359-7
  1. Wildlife wood-carving—Technique. 2. Birds in art. I. Title.
  TT199.7.B3575 2015
  736'.4—dc23
                                        2015027939

To Linda,
who has been with me
every step of the way

CONTENTS

FOREWORD

Reckoning with Barth

In 1990, the Cleveland Museum of Art sponsored the exhibition "Reckoning with Homer." The show explored the impact Winslow Homer's monumental turn-of-the-century seascapes had upon the next generations of artists who endeavored to paint the Maine coast. The curator's contention was that Homer's paintings of that landscape were so powerful that all future artists' interpretations started with the question, "Where do I go from Homer?"

Rembrandt Bugatti in Antwerp, John Singer Sargent in Venice, Thomas Moran in Yellowstone—each artist laid intimidating challenges to what later artists would need to see and interpret if they were to add to those icons' observations.

By 1991, at age thirty-four, Larry Barth had already been honored three times as the world champion at the Ward Foundation's Wildfowl Carving Competition. Our lives are overfull of "World Champion" designations. The casual attribution diminishes the currency. But Barth works have been honored a further thirteen times at that show. The honor is not casual; Larry's observations and skills have moved what was considered the folk craft of bird carving to artistic sculpture at its highest level. His is the work to be reckoned with by all artists interpreting birds in artistic media. Larry Barth's sculptures have set the artistic bar for our generation.

This book is a labor and a treasure. When an artist's life's work will be measured in a few dozen sculptures, time spent away from pursuing new ideas for future works is a significant decision. Only once, in 2003, was a large body of Barth's work assembled for a one-man show at the Mass Audubon's Visual Arts Center in Canton, Massachusetts. The overwhelming logistics, the fragility of the pieces, the difficulty of transportation, and the cajoling of lenders were overcome for four short months. The result was magical. The show was a midlife retrospective of Barth's work to date. This book has a different goal and a different power. A retrospective is a looking back. This book is about putting the artistic journey into perspective, giving insight into the decisions, events, and choices which have brought these works to creation. It is a look at a "Life of Careful and Joyful Observation."

I traveled to Canton to see the Mass Audubon show. Before me was a body of work displaying unparalleled levels of both carving skill and artistic courage. Courage? Sculpting in wood is a slow and methodical process. Even early compositional decisions in that medium are difficult to alter. The gestures of birds, particularly the species that hold Barth's attention, are very subtle. The difference between a convincing behavioral storyline and one that is confused or wrong can be measured in a millimeter's shift in head position or a centimeter's adjustment in foothold. The challenge of engineering the weightlessness of birds is daunting. One must convincingly lose all evidence of internal support while maintaining structural integrity. Casual observations of behavior or gesture do not survive the ruthless editing needed to move the carved work from merely competent modeling to fine sculpture. In the face of all these issues and required skills, you might expect a retrospective body of work simply showing the mastering of a handful of these problems and working with a limited palette of species and subjects.

Instead, in the Mass Audubon Gallery was a room of sculpture showing different subjects at different scales, masterfully crafted, addressing a wide range of sculptural and engineering challenges, all moving between storylines of great simplicity and powerful complexity. It was a room full of great artistic courage. The few potential failures had been worked through to appear effortlessly whole. There was sculpture that seemed unsculpted; there were engineering solutions to be marveled at in retrospect, artfully muted in the present; there were simple gestures elevated to elegant statements. Birds as birds: perfect, magical, and artful.

On Larry's studio wall is a small handwritten note: "To achieve all that is possible, we must attempt the impossible." Larry Barth's sculpture does seem impossible. That he has achieved the impossible without the technical aspects of the work overwhelming the viewers' experience is a measure of their success as sculpture.

All the possibility starts with joyful observation. Salman Rushdie, in a remembrance of Gabriel García Márquez and the South American literary genre of Magical Realism, observed that Márquez's "flights of fancy [worked because they had] real ground beneath them." Larry Barth's sculpture is Magical Realism. His flights of fancy are grounded in years of solid observation. His sketchbooks record thousands of the intimate situations, gestures, and anatomical details that give him the authority to edit his final compositions. A Barth sculpture is tight. From initial musings to finished work, everything unnecessary to the successful articulation of the idea is edited out of the final work. The elimination of the extraneous is a mark of a Barth. Pieces are spare; each element does real work. Each subtle shift in center of gravity, each distance and negative space, and each behavioral gesture moves the piece closer to a perfection that releases the viewer from any thought of biological analysis. They are Birds as Art.

In 1991, Larry Barth was honored by the Leigh Yawkey Woodson Art Museum in Wausau, Wisconsin, as a Master Wildlife Artist. The honor is part of the museum's "Birds in Art" annual exhibition and celebration. Within the bird art community this honor is coveted and its importance understood. Barth was chosen as a Master to join a very small and select alumnae including Roger Tory Peterson, Fenwick Lansdowne, Sir Peter Scott, and Robert Bateman. He was the youngest person to be so honored. He was the first and only representational wood sculptor. He was the first person so honored from an artistic tradition that occupied a netherland between folk craft and fine art. The museum acknowledged that Barth's skills and vision were truly unique. His sculptural accomplishments of the following twenty-plus years have only strengthened the prescience of the museum's decision.

In 1789, the Reverend Gilbert White published *The Natural History of Selborne*, a collection of letters detailing a calendar of small biological observations. Any one observation, while interesting, is not related to past observations. It is only in reading through the years of the letters that one puts together a vivid understanding of the ecology and environmental conditions of the County of Southampton in the late 1700s. For years, Larry and I have shared a series of phone calls noting the biological arrival of spring. The calls are a casual, unrecorded version of a Natural History of Stahlstown, Pennsylvania, and Dickerson, Maryland. On the surface, nothing important is discussed. Conversations move from mourning cloak butterflies flying over snowfields to the dates of the first singing phoebe of the year to the internal biology of the wood frog. The rambling musings are footnotes of an ephemeral season. I believe they are also at the heart of Barth's art. To me, they are a continual reminder of just how passionately and comprehensively he lives his work. His art is built on disciplined observation. This book is a celebration of these observations and the talent that brought them to life with knife and brush.

Walt Matia
April 2015

ACKNOWLEDGMENTS

There are so many to thank. I begin with my parents, for I owe my start to them. My mother's interest in birds and my father's in carving are both manifest in me and in my work. It is clear that what I do and who I am comes from them. I could not have had a better start in life.

Family and friends have encouraged and helped me in countless ways. I am especially grateful to Tom Duran, Jeff Leonhardt, Clint Knupp, Bob Shamey, Paul Sirofchuck, Tim TerMeer, and Gigi Hopkins for the hands-on assistance they have so generously provided.

Three dear friends, John Scheeler, Bob Guge, and John Walker, are no longer with us, but they will always be with me. I miss them and the chance to share this book with them. Each has left a void in my life with his passing.

No artist is self-taught. I have benefited from the work of all the artists whose work I have been privileged to see. Some I have only known through their work; many I have had the pleasure of knowing personally as well. I'll mention just two by name, Louis Agassiz Fuertes and Don Richard Eckelberry, whose work had a great impact on me during the early days while I was laying the foundational links in place that helped me connect with birds and with art. Fuertes's work made me want to paint birds. Eckelberry's work made me want to carve them. Beyond these two, it

simply becomes a list of everyone who carves, sculpts, and paints.

Three institutions deserve special thanks for so graciously providing access to the work I have in their collections so those pieces could be photographed: the Ward Foundation and the Ward Museum of Wildfowl Art directed by Lora Bottinelli, the Leigh Yawkey Woodson Art Museum directed by Kathy Foley, and Mass Audubon's Museum of American Bird Art directed by Amy Montague. These three museums have become as important to me personally as they have been to my work. I am truly grateful to each of them, and to their directors and staff, for all they have done.

Ysbrand Brouwers and the Artists for Nature Foundation have given me opportunities in the field to work with and know new places and artists that have enriched my life and my work.

Carnegie Museum of Natural History's Section of Birds and Powdermill Nature Reserve have been tremendous resources during all the years that I have been carving. Bob Leberman and Bob Mulvihill, whom I will continue to think of as *the* banders at Powdermill, deserve special mention and thanks.

Carnegie Mellon University played a part in helping me find my artistic footing. I will always be grateful to the nameless interviewer in the painting and sculpture department who, after viewing my portfolio, told me I would get in, but I wouldn't be happy there and I should go see the design people. It was the most valuable career counseling I ever received. The design department became my home for four years. I learned as much from my fellow design students as I did from our professors—thoughts, memories, lessons, and guidance from those years long ago continue to arise unbidden with surprising frequency.

None of this works without the support of my patrons, the people and institutions that didn't have to purchase my work and yet have elected to do so. I am grateful to Kirk and Nellie Williams, Andy and Sandy Andrews, Eldridge and Peg Arnold, Sandor Garfinkle, Gary and Barbara Grendys, Roger Jones, Giovanni and Cecilia Lamenza, Doug Miller, Thomas H. Nimick, Katie and Donal O'Brien, Charles and Susan Snyder, Bert and Leigh Tuckey, and many others for their tangible interest in my work.

Judith Schnell's interest in my work and persistence in wanting this book to happen is, in fact, what has made it happen. I am grateful to her and to the people at Stackpole for providing a means for my work to be seen.

Walter Matia has been an especially good friend over many years, and I am grateful to him for such an eloquent foreword. I wish he could have written the rest of the book as well. I think of Walt every time I pause in the evening to listen to the Wood Thrushes, knowing that in all likelihood he is doing the same.

My life and my work are one and the same, which means that my wife, Linda, my son, Eric, and my daughter, Emily, have always been a part of what I do. I like it that way and I am grateful to each of them for being as involved as they have been. Eric has always been able to tell me when a piece is done. Emily has always had a knack for asking the right questions. And of all the people on this earth, Linda is the one with whom I have always been most eager to share whatever successes that I, or more accurately *we*, have had. She is the first person I will want to see this book.

—*Larry Barth*

INTRODUCTION

For years I was reluctant to commit to the idea of writing a book about my work. I didn't feel I had a large enough body of work to merit such an endeavor, and I did not feel I was in a position to speak with authority about matters as weighty and powerful as art. It seemed to me that the best use of my time was to work on my next big piece. The work itself seemed more important than a book about it. But over time my perspective has changed. With each piece I've gained experience, insight, and confidence. I am now to the point where I am comfortable with the ongoing artistic struggle rather than being overwhelmed by it. I have begun to think of a book not as something keeping me from my work, but as a vital part of it. A book serves as a record of what I've learned along the way as I have sought to find my place in the world of art and design. In a very real sense, the book itself has become one of my pieces.

One of the biggest challenges in doing this book was finding an effective way to use two-dimensional images to represent three-dimensional objects. I have been aware of this concern all my life. Even when I was young, I knew that the large rectangular 2-D *Map of the World* that hung on the classroom wall was flawed. The standard Mercator projection made Greenland look bigger than South America and represented Antarctica with an odd white band running across the bottom. The globe on the other side of the classroom was better,

but I still couldn't see the whole thing without physically giving it a spin or walking around to the other side. The same is true with my sculpture. The best way to view it is by moving around it in person. This book offers the next best thing to seeing the work in person. Many images of each piece provide different views and angles to give you a sense of the piece as whole, and tighter shots allow you to "lean in" to get a closer look. This is the most thorough two-dimensional representation that my three-dimensional work has ever had.

Not every piece I've done has been included in this book—far from it. The pieces I have selected show the range of my work and mark significant milestones in my development as a sculptor. Many are pivotal pieces that were key in my taking design and presentation in new and different directions.

My goal in doing the book is to share my work and also the thought behind it. The text includes enough information about the process to allow a basic understanding of the techniques I use to bring a piece into being. The overall focus of the book, however, is on what I do and why I do it, rather than on how it is done. I have tried to honestly and candidly talk about how a piece comes together, including what didn't work as well as what did, because both are part of working out a composition. With each piece I do, I continue to refine my thinking about the things that matter to me: birds, art, and design.

WINTER LAKESHORE

Snowy Owl & Bonaparte's Gull

Moving beyond craft

I like birds. I always have. My strongest memories from very early childhood are of birds—a white gull overhead against a blue sky; the bounding gait of an injured flicker underneath the shrubbery; pattern showing in the wings of ducks lifting off from a bend in the river; the iridescence of a dead hummingbird; the bold black, white, and magenta of a rose-breasted grosbeak up close; and the stateliness of a great blue heron in the distance. These memories are not hazy or vague. They are clear and focused, filled with vivid detail.

Birds have always had my full attention. I am drawn in by the rich tapestry of detail that I see in a single bird, and I'm taken aback by the rich variety I see in birds as a whole. I marvel at their perfection. Of all the designs I see in nature, I find the shapes, colors, and patterns of birds to be the most beautiful.

Given their perfection, I choose to present the birds as they are, without distortion or modification. It is also no surprise that I feel compelled to include so much of the detail in which I take delight and pleasure. The faithful realism you see in my treatment of the bird itself has been a constant in my work. It is in the ever-changing compositions I build *around* the birds

that you will see considerable variation. I use birds to explore art. The bird is a given. It is in the arena of design, composition, and presentation that I fight my battles, pursue new ideas, embrace aesthetics, look for opportunities, take chances, try alternatives, and investigate the possibilities that come as I bend, spindle, fold, and manipulate my way down the artistic path.

Winter Lakeshore was conceived at a time when prevailing convention in carving dictated that a bird be perched on some bit of branch or habitat centered on a lathe-turned base. And while there is potential for excellence in that format, too often the result was just a bird on a stick on a base. Bird carvings tended to be three-dimensional vignettes, constrained portraits that did not expand visually to fill any more space than what they physically occupied. I am not separating myself from this trend, for I was a part of it, but I had long felt that the *craft* of bird carving had the potential to become the *art* of bird sculpture. My instincts, coupled with my fine-art training, have led me to conclude that the key to realizing bird carving's potential lies in how the work is presented. It is a question of thoughtful design rather than technical skill.

Snowy Owls are birds of the far north. Occasionally, population dynamics cause them to disperse southward. When they move outside their normal range, they favor open country similar to their tundra home. In an "invasion" year, it would not be unusual for a Snowy Owl to spend the winter among the dunes on the shores of the Great Lakes.

The base, or more accurately, the absence of a base, was crucial to the success of *Winter Lakeshore*. I used the flow of grass and sand to establish a mood and atmosphere that could provide context for the bird. I wanted to make the piece more than just a portrait of an owl: I wanted to give the viewer a fuller sense of being there on that beach. By eliminating any sort of formal, turned base and extending the feathered edge of the sand out onto the table surface, I invite the viewer to mentally fill in the expanse of beach surrounding the piece. The space around the piece becomes as meaningful as the piece itself—what isn't there ends up having as much presence as what is. The owl's line of sight becomes a tangible element in the composition. The bird's gaze works in tandem with the extended spit of sand to suggest a continuation that moves well beyond the piece. You can relate to the bird because you, too, know what it's like to look down the length of a long, empty beach toward a distant horizon.

Winter Lakeshore
27 x 26 x 48
acrylic on basswood
1985

The process

Those who are unfamiliar with my work may find it difficult to know exactly what it is they are seeing. Once a piece is painted, it can be hard to tell that the birds are carved out of wood or that the plants are made of metal. To make the finished work more accessible, it's helpful to have a basic understanding of the tools, techniques, and materials involved in the process. I believe the artistic content of the finished work is more important than the process, but in truth, the art and the craft are tied together. Neither can be fully understood without the context provided by the other.

Everything I do starts with observation and moves quickly to paper. I rely heavily on field work. Almost without exception, each piece is based on a personal experience that I have had with a live bird in the field or, if possible, in the hand. I record my observations with a pencil and sketchbook. I learned a long time ago that I am a far better observer with a sketchbook than I am with a camera. With a camera, I tend to take the shot and move on. I tell myself I can study it later when there is more time. Sketching forces me to slow down, look harder, and study the subject while it is still in front of me.

In the field I sketch what I see. Back in the studio I make drawings that reflect what I'm thinking about, which usually includes the images I have brought back from the field. From the sketches, ideas grow and develop and eventually become subjects for sculpture.

Snowy Owl
drawn from a captive bird
Pittsburgh Aviary
October 20, 1984

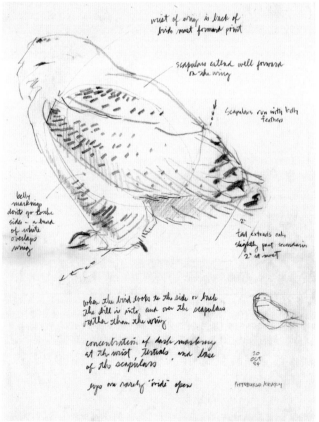

When I have taken an idea as far as I can on paper, it is time to move into three dimensions. I start in clay and work out the pose of every bird I carve with a full-sized model. In the early years I used plasticine, an oil-based clay that never hardens. I still use plasticine for larger projects, but I now make most of my models out of polymer clay, which can be fired at low temperatures and made permanent. In clay, I concentrate on the essence of the bird—its overall attitude, stance, and gesture. My clay birds are accurate but not detailed. The big decisions, such as the axis of the bird's body, the turn of a head, or the angle of a tail, are made in clay, where changes are more easily made than in wood.

Once I am satisfied with the clay model, I move to wood. I carve my birds in either basswood or tupelo. I prefer basswood, but will use tupelo in certain circumstances. Tupelo is much lighter than basswood, which can make it the better choice when weight is a concern. (Weight is always a concern with birds in flight.)

Using the clay model as a pattern and guide, I rough out the bird with chisels. Properly sharpened chisels are a joy to use. I prefer them over power tools that grind the wood away and fill the air with dust. All of my birds are carved out of solid blocks. There are no inserted feathers. Birds in flight are an exception—open wings are carved separately, but each wing is still carved as one piece out of a single block. When I rough out a bird, my first priority is to establish the relationship of the head to the body. Once the head is in place, I work to determine the location of the eyes. I set the glass eyes in place as early as possible, often on the first day.

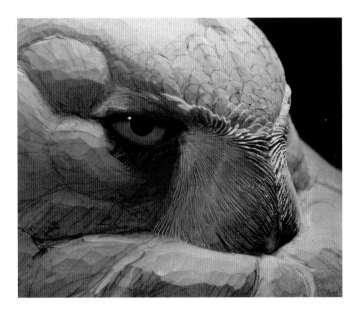

Top: Roughing out alongside the clay model
Middle: One-piece open wing
Bottom: Head detail with glass eyes in place

7

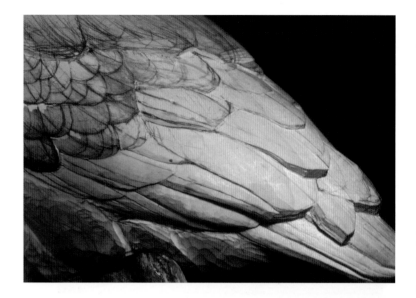

Continuing with chisels, I work from large shapes to smaller ones, and eventually to individual feathers. I draw and redraw the feathers countless times, making adjustments and trying different arrangements until I get a feather layout that pleases me. Chisels lend themselves to my geometric approach to shaping a bird. I work as geometrically as possible for as long as possible. Feathers and feather groups start out as planes, levels, and terraces separated by bold steps and staircases. Working this way, I am better able to gauge the heights and distances between neighboring groups. I also believe some of the power and boldness in the strong, angular shapes and planes that result from working with chisels remain even after the angles and edges have been eased into softer, rounded feather shapes. I see the surface of a bird as a landscape with ridges, valleys, gentle slopes, rising hills, and rivers that carry your eye from one area of interest to the next.

I do very little sanding. Each feather is shaved down to its final form with flat chisels and skews.

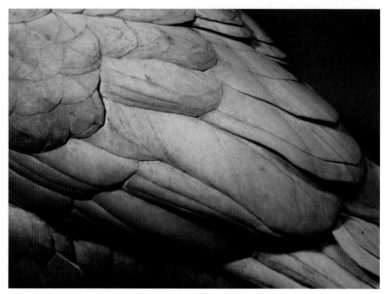

The feather splits are composed in groups and carved with a small V-shaped chisel. I place splits carefully to take advantage of contrasting lights and darks in the bird's plumage that will not show up until the bird is painted. I save undercuts for last because once a feather is undercut, its position is fixed and it can no longer be moved. With the shape of the bird fully resolved—down to each individual feather—and lightly sanded, the bird is ready for texture.

Top: Roughing out the wing
Middle: Feathers carved and undercut
Bottom: Ready for texture, sanded smooth, feather splits in place

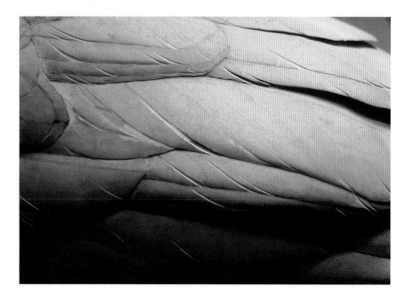

I revisit each feather I have carved and give it an appropriate texture with one of two different methods: burning or grinding. For the well-defined feathers with distinct, hard edges, I use a woodburner. The burning pen has a temperature-controlled, angled, pointed tip. I use it to burn in the shaft of the feather and then for each of the individual parallel lines that radiate out from along the shaft to form the vane. It is a slow, tedious task, but one that I enjoy immensely. For the first time, the surface of the bird starts to look more like feathers than wood.

When the feathers are soft and more loosely defined, I use a small-diameter stone cylinder in a high-speed hand piece to grind in the texture. Grinding is not as precise as burning, making it appropriate for the softer areas of the bird such as the breast and underparts, where the feathers can be almost like hair or fur.

Once the bird has been fully textured, sealed, and primed with gesso, it's ready for paint. I use acrylics. Using a museum study skin as a reference for color and pattern, I start at the tail and work forward to the bill, painting the feathers in the same order in which they overlap on the real bird. I paint quickly. I need to get in and out fast to avoid clogging the surface detail and to keep the paint from becoming too thick and shiny. A healthy sheen is okay, but shine is too much. Painting is easily the most intense and difficult part of the entire process. It's exhilarating when it goes well, but devastating when it doesn't.

Top: Burned feather texture
Middle: Ground feather texture
Bottom: Painting alongside museum study skin

The unexpected length of the extended toe of sand calls attention to itself. But there is nothing there, no detail to hold your eye. So your eye moves to the center of interest: the birds. From there, everything doubles back upon the sand. The owl gazes down the spit; the grasses flow toward the tip. The gull's wing wraps around the back and reaches forward; the driftwood folds back upon itself. Everything takes you back to the beginning and sets you up for another run. Your eye is constantly moving, but moving within the piece, not away from it.

Repeating shapes and rhythms throughout a piece builds continuity and helps tie it together visually. But it's a subtle business—too much repetition becomes monotony, and repetition that is too obvious appears contrived. The tactic seems to work best when the examples are almost hidden. Shapes can be repeated discreetly throughout a piece in such a way that the unifying effect is noticed but the individual examples are not. The viewer can tell if the various elements in a composition are working together without necessarily being aware of why they work or how they work, or what has been done to achieve a pleasing balance.

The end of the driftwood repeats the shape of the owl's tail above it. This is especially evident in the photo on page 4, where the lines and angles of the tail and driftwood are nearly identical. The tips of the gull's wings are repeated on the other side of the bird in the driftwood. The owl balances over two gulls, a wooden one on the left and a feathered one on the right. The shape of the gull's open wing is repeated in the shape of the sand. Each has a deckled edge, formed by individual feathers in the bird and repeated with the ridges in the rippled sand. Although subtle, these compositional devices make important contributions to the unified whole.

The diminutive Bonaparte's Gull was chosen for its size in relation to the owl (most gulls are surprisingly large) and because of the likelihood that it and a Snowy Owl would frequent the same inland beach. Snowy Owls can vary, from being heavily marked to almost pure white. Gulls can, too. Because I chose to present the owl as a heavily barred individual, I gave the gull the clean, unmarked plumage of a winter adult. Had I chosen to present an owl with plumage closer to pure white, I would have used the more heavily patterned plumage of an immature gull. Repetition can be a good thing in a composition, but there is a time and a place for contrast as well. Contrast—used at the right time, in the right place, and in the right way—is what keeps repetition from becoming monotonous. The contrast of the cool, clear gray of the gull set against the warm, patterned white of the owl makes the area where the birds are joined more easily understood by giving more distinction to the individual birds.

At least some small part of the gull is visible from any angle. It teases you, always providing a hint that beckons you to come around the piece and view it from the other side. And when you move around to see the gull better and it has your full attention, you don't notice that the back of the owl's head has no features, because the gull has taken center stage. Your eye continues to rove, and the owl's eyes call you back. Face to face. Eye to eye. Moving. Moving. Always moving.

12

A bird at rest need not be dull.
Design and composition can animate
a piece and create movement.

TERNS IN FLIGHT

Common Terns

The importance of presentation

Years ago I came across a statement by Leopold Blaschka, the elder of a father-and-son team that spent almost fifty years creating an incredible collection of glass flowers for Harvard University. Blaschka said that art could be anything done with uncommon skill, tact, and finesse. I like how his statement places the emphasis on the concept of potential. It alludes to the possibilities of what *can* be art rather than declaring what art *is*. I, too, feel that almost any endeavor carries the *potential* to become art. Achieving that potential is not easy. Nor should it be, for if art is to maintain *its* fullest potential, the bar must be set very high.

I think that carving birds can go as far as anyone is able to take it. I will take it as far as I can with the skills and abilities I bring to bear in my ongoing attempts to move toward art. Whether I achieve my artistic goals or not, I feel the goals themselves bring a certain focus and integrity to the effort. For me, art is both the journey and the destination.

Terns in Flight was completed in 1986. All through the 1980s, bird carving was on the rise. The number of carvers and shows was growing steadily. Competitions were packed with carvers, carvings, vendors, merchants, suppliers, buyers, sellers, collectors, and a captivated public. It seemed that everyone involved was convinced that bird carving was an "art form." I was not so sure. Seeing the work crammed together on folding tables lined up in gymnasiums and convention halls was not how I felt art should be presented. In museum and gallery settings, sculpture is offered to the viewer on an appropriate pedestal. Each piece is given the space it deserves, commensurate with its stature and importance.

I believed in the potential of bird carving. At the same time, I was aware of the distance between where it could go and where it was. I wanted the work to be lifted up, to be seen in its best light, to be seen as sculpture. In order for that to happen, the manner in which the birds were being presented needed to be as elegant as the birds themselves. In my previous effort, *Winter Lakeshore*, I had sought to break away from the conventional look of bird carving by eliminating the base. With *Terns in Flight*, I had the same intention, but this time I took the exact opposite approach. Instead of eliminating the base, I made it more formal than ever. The base became the pedestal that would be consistent with a finer venue. It introduced an artful poise and dignity that I felt was missing from bird carving. By incorporating a pedestal into the design of the piece, I was better able to control how the piece would be seen. Whether displayed in a museum or somewhere less austere, the work needed to be presented well.

16

Terns in Flight
45 x 15 x 17
acrylic on basswood
1986

If you want to move beyond craft while being involved in an endeavor that makes extensive use of craftsmanship, then you must find ways to take the craftsmanship out of the spotlight.

This may seem counterintuitive, but craftsmanship becomes less of an issue the better it is done. When something is done really, really well, people are less inclined to notice the effort involved. A skilled performer makes it look easy. When the execution is flawless, people focus directly on the result.

Poorly executed craftsmanship calls attention to itself and becomes difficult to ignore. Good craftsmanship drops out of sight and clears the way for appreciating what has been achieved. If I can eliminate every burr, every roughness, every imperfection, so that the viewer's eye roams over the piece smoothly without hanging up on any small blemish, defect, or flaw, then the viewer is more inclined to perceive the whole rather than the parts . . . to perceive the design of the piece rather than the execution, to see the art rather than the craft.

The pedestal base raises the birds up to eye level and reinforces the vertical format of the composition. It gives the piece height without calling attention to how that height was achieved. Its simple geometry and lack of detail are immediately and completely understood, allowing the viewer to move straight to the main subject: the terns. The black base provides a sculptural solution that looks clean, modern, and contemporary while at the same time appearing classic and traditional. It is an elegant solution that taps into the strengths of both looks. I enjoy the contrast of the base's rigid geometry in relation to the subtle, organic curves found in the birds. It can be difficult to appreciate the exact nature of a single gentle curve when that curve is set among other similar curves, but if that same curve is set against a perfectly straight edge, its subtle beauty is starkly revealed. The terns' shapes and curves set against the square, black base seem all the more delicate and exquisite. The top of the base is faceted into the suggestion of the sea—just enough to carry the idea and place the birds in context, but not too much because the more important element is the air itself. The space the birds are moving through is more important than the water they are moving over.

I maintained control of the many lines and angles in *Terns in Flight* by relating the lines inside the piece to a point outside the piece.

The two lower wings form lines that converge on a point below and behind the birds (a point close to the lower left corner of this page). As the wing lines of the two birds move out and away from that point, they gently diverge. (Think of them as the shape of each bird reduced to a single zigzag line, like a child's drawing of a seagull.) Moving up through the piece, the distances between the corresponding parts of the two birds increase steadily. The piece gently blossoms upward and outward. The lines spiral up, unwinding like a coiled spring releasing tension.

The lower bird's high wingtip curves up just enough to bring the diverging lines back together. Its recurve swings your eye up to reconnect with the high wingtip of the upper tern, and from there your eye drifts back down through the core of the piece.

THE WOOD WARBLERS

Family Parulidae

A bird in the hand

Again and again, I am struck with the flawless beauty of birds. During my time in the field, I may encounter something that moves me so deeply I cannot help but respond. My response is an effort to better and more fully understand what I have seen. I want to hold on to the image as long as I can to somehow make it mine. Art is my way of taking possession of the beauty I see in the natural world. Art has helped me further the relationship I enjoy with birds, and I have come to realize that birds have been my means of exploring art, and that art, in and of itself, is just as important to me as the birds are. Each has enhanced my understanding of the other, and in my work the two have become one.

I find the members of the family Parulidae, the New World or Wood Warblers, to be particularly attractive. Unfortunately, warblers can be easy to miss. They are quite small, not much bigger than sparrows, and often move through the treetops unnoticed, either too high or too hidden to be seen well. From a distance, they appear as little more than unremarkable dark silhouettes. Francis Lee Jaques, an artist who favored nature's design on a grander scale, is credited with having said, "The difference between warblers and no warblers is very slight." It takes some intentional

effort to get to know the warblers, but once properly introduced, the same birds that were once so easy to overlook become impossible to ignore. A good look through binoculars transforms those treetop silhouettes into bright jewels. Suddenly, a dazzling world of hidden treasure is revealed.

My effort to get to know these birds better included moving close to Powdermill Nature Reserve. Powdermill is the Carnegie Museum of Natural History's 2,200-acre field station, located in southwestern Pennsylvania, and features a bird banding program that has operated year-round since 1961. The bird banders at Powdermill capture birds, collect and record data, and place numbered bands on the birds' legs. The birds are then released, unharmed. Recovering a band is a bonus, but the real value is in the recorded data. And so it is for me as well. The information I have been able to gather at Powdermill has been invaluable. I've been able to work from life—to study, take notes, and sketch from live, handheld birds. The opportunity to hold warblers and other birds, to examine them so closely and see them so well, has had a profound impact on my work. Interacting with birds in such an intimate way is moving. It stirs my blood. Having seen and held the live bird, how can I help but respond?

In the Sycamores
Parula Warbler
19 x 8 x 8
Yellow-throated Warbler
18 x 8 x 8
acrylic on basswood
1987

In the Tamaracks
Black-throated Green Warbler
20 x 9 x 7
Black-and-white Warbler
21 x 7 x 5
acrylic on basswood
1986

Ovenbird
drawn from a handheld bird
Powdermill Nature Reserve
April 30, 1992

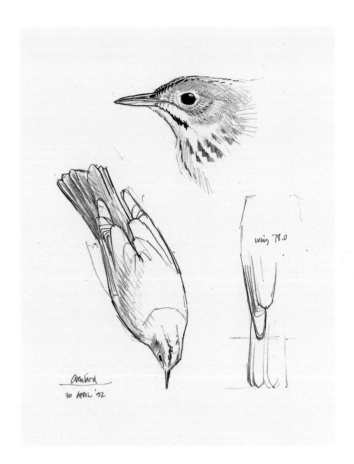

The bird banding program at Powdermill Nature Reserve was established by Robert C. Leberman in 1961. I first visited Powdermill in 1971. Ten years later, in 1981, I moved within five miles of Powdermill. And shortly after that, I moved to where I am now, just a mile and a half away. This gradual convergence indicates just how important Powdermill has been to me and my work. Simply put, Powdermill has enabled me to work from life so that I could put life in my work.

Powdermill gives me the opportunity to know the birds I love more intimately. To hold live birds, to feel their strength and fragility, to see and feel the way they move, has more value than I can say. The way a foot grasps my finger, the way an eye moves and changes the shape of a face, the way a folded wing conforms to a body . . . every bit of information, every observation, every sketch, has contributed to a deeper and fuller understanding of birds.

The banders, Bob Leberman and Bob Mulvihill, have been far more than just knowledgeable—they've been good friends who have accommodated me in every way. Many, many times they have caught the bird I was working on exactly when a live model could do the most good.

While I have, on different occasions, modeled, sculpted, carved, and painted all directly from live birds, my primary tool has been my sketchbook.

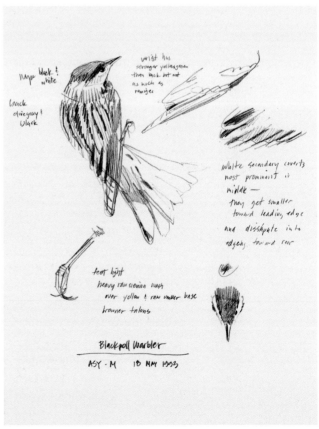

Blackpoll Warbler
drawn from a handheld bird
Powdermill Nature Reserve
May 18, 1993

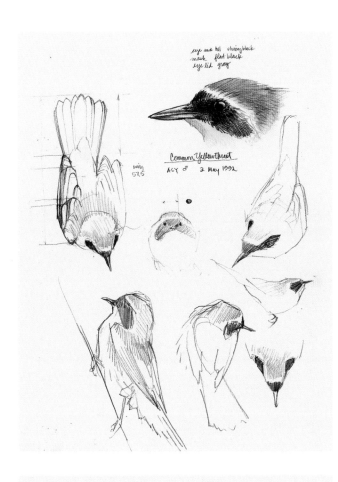

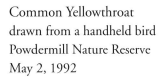

Common Yellowthroat
drawn from a handheld bird
Powdermill Nature Reserve
May 2, 1992

My Powdermill sketches are slightly different from the sketches I produce in the field. They usually include grid-like hash marks that indicate measurements I have taken. At Powdermill, I don't get the bird until it has already been through the banding process. The bird cannot be held indefinitely, so I must work quickly. I concentrate on a few basic measurements, such as the wing length, the relationship of the wing to the tail, and the distance between the eyes. I spend what time I have left noting details. I pay particular attention to faces, especially the eyes themselves. Color notes—especially for eyes, bills, and feet—are important and can be useful later on.

The most important thing to do is simply look. Careful observation is the very first step of everything I do.

Black-and-white Warbler
drawn from a handheld bird
Powdermill Nature Reserve
no date

Warblers travel in groups. During migration, it is not unusual to come upon a wave of birds that may contain a dozen or more different species. It's thrilling to find yourself in the middle of such an encounter. Suddenly, the trees are alive with birds, and there is something new and exciting in every direction. You want to savor each one, but you don't want to miss the others. The birds spin you around—you can't look fast enough as you try to take in the visual feast.

As I contemplated how I could present warblers sculpturally, I thought about ways to include the dynamics of such an experience. It seemed to me that one bird alone could hardly convey the variety and vitality of warblers as a whole. The idea of presenting pairs of mixed species took hold. This enabled me to not only offer up the singular beauty of the individual birds, but also hint at the visual excitement of warblers as a group. In each mixed pair, the individual birds are presented independently. Each one stands on its own, complete and whole. But when the pair is brought together, a new whole is created—a whole that is greater than the sum of its parts and can say something more than the individual components could say by themselves.

In the Sycamores and *In the Tamaracks* both unite two different warblers. In each case, the habitat ties the species together. The interplay between the repeated lines seen in the two variations of sycamore or tamarack, along with the matching bases, provides the unifying elements that hold the pairs together.

When I started composing these pieces, the proportions were far different than they are now. I struggled with scale. I started out by placing the small birds on small branches. That seemed reasonable, but it didn't work. The birds did not look right. Even though my carved warblers *were* small, they didn't appear to be. The problem was not the birds, but rather the branches. It took me a while to include as much branch as the pieces have now. Initially, I was concerned that larger branches would overpower the small birds. I found the opposite to be true. When I increased the size of the branches, the birds were not overwhelmed: they were put into context. The branches, in fact, *had* to dwarf the birds in order for the birds to be seen properly. The warblers did not look small *unless* and *until* they were dwarfed by their surroundings, just as they are in nature.

Sycamores are common in Pennsylvania and are often the dominant trees along the state's streams and rivers. Younger trees are somewhat uniform, but older trees develop quite a bit of character. Old bark peels off in irregular sheets, exposing new patches of fresh color, and branches develop elegant, calligraphic lines that arc unexpectedly to the left or right. The character of the branches seems to extend all the way out to the very tips. Lower branches descend and fall with graceful flourishes and lovely, curving lines.

I chose to present a Parula Warbler with a Yellow-throated Warbler. While neither species requires an aquatic habitat, they both seem to have an affinity for water and can be found in the same streamside setting. I've seen both species together along the stream that passes next to my studio. Parula Warblers nest close to my studio every year. They have a distinctive song that rises up slowly and then drops with an abrupt finish. I listen for it every time I step outside. Perhaps the fact that I hear the bird more often than I see it led me to present a singing bird.

Even though I don't have any sycamores on my property, it was easy enough to imagine the birds in a streamside setting that included them. The beauty of the birds combines well with the eloquence and grace of the sycamore's attractive branches.

On rare occasions, Parula and Yellow-throated Warblers have been known to breed together, producing a hybrid known as Sutton's Warbler. *In the Sycamores* is a subtle tribute to the possibility of a Sutton's Warbler and is based on a similar if not identical relationship: two independent species that complement each other and together can become something more.

Sutton's Warbler is named for the man who discovered it, George Miksch Sutton (1898–1982), a bird artist and man of science whose work I have long admired. Though I never met him, I've always felt a connection to him. He worked for a number of years at the Carnegie Museum of Natural History in Pittsburgh and had a hand in some of the dioramas that would fuel my interest in birds years later and start me on a path toward three dimensions. He prepared the best museum study skins I have ever seen. Many times I've had the privilege of working with Sutton's skins and have been acutely aware of the fact that, aside from the years that separate us, we have both handled and admired the exact same specimen. I can no longer meet the man, but I keep looking in the sycamores. Perhaps one day I will see his warbler.

The drooping branches of tamarack are beautiful with or without their needles. I placed the more colorful Black-throated Green Warbler on a branch without needles; the bird's colorful plumage makes up for the lack of color in the bare branch. In the companion piece, I reversed the color role and set the black-and-white bird against a needled branch. Its neutral plumage offers nothing to compete with the green needles that enliven the branch and the piece. In each composition, color is paired with neutrality in the opposite way. When the two pieces that form the pair are brought together, each offers a variation that complements the other. The pieces became a pair through composition rather than simple repetition.

Just as with *In the Sycamores*, I had a subtle reason for *In the Tamaracks'* pairing. The first warbler I found and identified on my own was a Black-throated Green. For me, it will always be a special bird. It reminds me of those powerful days of my youth when the excitement of discovering everything for the first time was almost unbearable. And the Black-and-white Warbler is my favorite bird, one that thrills me every single time I see it. In my mind, these two special birds are especially fitting companions.

I never thought of myself as having a favorite bird. I liked too many birds for too many reasons to pick just one. If pressed, I was likely to say the one I was currently working on was my favorite. It was, after all, the one holding my complete and undivided attention at the time.

That all changed the first time I held a Black-and-white Warbler at Powdermill. I had seen Black-and-whites many times before, but getting one in hand at the banding lab was like seeing it for the first time. It was the undertail coverts that got me. The feathers underneath the tail are not always evident on a bird in the field, but they were easy to see on the one I held. Clean black arrows hugged the tightly curved radiuses of the small coverts so perfectly it made me wince. As I looked over the rest of the bird, I realized it had all of my favorite markings—crown stripes, a clean eye ring, wing bars, tail spots, edged tertials, a streaked back and belly, and those perfect immaculate tail coverts—all put together with grace and style. The Black-and-white Warbler has since become my favorite bird. As an added bonus, black and white is a favorite color scheme of mine. Not everyone would consider it a *color* scheme, but I do. As a sculptor, I've always felt a strong graphic pattern can have just as much visual impact as strong color, maybe even more.

The Wood Warblers are a very special group.
Perfectly patterned and proportioned, they are
exquisite examples of the perfection I see in birds.

IN THE HEMLOCKS

Blackburnian Warblers

"Beauty is its own excuse for being." —Ralph Waldo Emerson

As I watch a brook trout holding its position in a clear mountain stream, a red eft pausing on its way across a patch of moss to survey its miniature world, or a luna moth resting quietly on the weathered siding of my studio, I am struck with just how perfect—and I do mean perfect—each one of these small bits of creation is: so perfect it almost hurts. And it occurs to me that none of these exquisite creatures has any idea how truly perfect it is: *that* is exactly what enables each to seem so very perfect. There is something about their lack of awareness of their own perfection that draws me to them. Our self-awareness can get in the way; if we think we might be perfect, then we most likely are not. The trout, the eft, and the moth don't think it— they just are. Their complete and total lack of awareness of just how magnificent they are is why they are so much closer to perfection than we are. In a moment shared with such perfection, I sense that I am somehow very close to a deep and profound truth, one that is exciting and at the same time humbling. If I can tap into that truth in any way, then I am on the right path.

Ultimately, art is a search for truth. I find truth in the beauty and perfection I see in the natural world, and I revel in it. The hemlocks that rise over my trout stream and the warblers that move among their graceful boughs—in their presence I am humbled. A Blackburnian Warbler illuminated by a shaft of light in a shady grove of hemlock fills me with reverent awe. Beauty is its own excuse for being.

In the Hemlocks followed a series of smaller pieces. I move back and forth between extremes. After working on a large and elaborate piece, I want to do something small and simple. And then, after several smaller pieces, I want to sink my teeth into another big one. I had just completed four small pieces designed to be presented in pairs (*In the Sycamores* and *In the Tamaracks*). The birds were similar enough to work side by side, but not in the same piece. They formed compositional pairs rather than mated biological pairs. Inevitably, I began to envision another pair of warblers, not as companion pieces but together in one larger piece. Presenting a pair of Blackburnian Warblers, male and female, would justify scaling up the setting as well. The larger format would allow me to expand the habitat even further, enabling it to play a major role in the composition.

In the Hemlocks would not have come about if not for the work that came before it. The journey is progressive and ongoing. Each piece reveals something new, and each effort leads to and influences the next.

In the Hemlocks
35 x 15 x 17
acrylic on basswood
1987

The decision to place the birds in Eastern Hemlock was an easy one. First and foremost is the fact that the birds themselves choose it. Blackburnians are found in a variety of conifers—not exclusively, but they favor hemlock with enough regularity that the two are a classic combination. I like it, too. The graceful, airy fall of a feathery hemlock bough appeals to me far more than the regular, orderly, upright growth of spruce. I've always favored plants with irregular growth patterns. I see more interesting possibilities for composition with shapes that are variable rather than fixed.

The casual presentation of the branch is very intentional. The branch descends from above, appearing to have been snapped off so recently that you can still sense the rest of the tree. The fine line of the bright green cambium layer still shows between the outer bark and the clean, light wood exposed by the fresh break. It barely touches the black base; the only contact is with a wisp of petticoat lace that peeks out from under a flowing skirt of dark green needles. I kept the connection to a minimum to maintain an airy lightness that enables the viewer to envision the branch at any height. Hemlock cones are small and delicate—fittingly proportioned to accompany the small, delicate warblers. Their tendency to grow singly or in small, loose clusters made it easy to create a cascade that moved through the bough from the high male bird down to the female below.

I see birds two ways: in the field and in the hand. In my sculpture, I present the birds in context. I want to show them the way they appeared to me in the field. I want to capitalize on the impact the birds have when seen against a backdrop of dark green hemlock.

I've also had the opportunity to handle the live birds at the banding lab and to carefully examine them very, very closely. With the bird in hand, the detail becomes more important than the context. Up close, I see things I never could from a distance. I get lost in a world of feather detail, an exquisite tapestry of intricate color, pattern, and texture.

I'd like my sculpture to offer the viewer the advantages provided by both of the ways I see birds. Viewing my work from a distance, I want you to be filled with the same sense of delight that I feel seeing birds in the field. And then, as you approach the piece more closely, I want you to be rewarded in the same way that I feel rewarded when I have a bird in my hand.

All of my work involves detail, but *In the Hemlocks* seems to contain significantly more than the usual amount. I felt it needed to, in order to capture and convey the essence of what I found so beautiful and attractive in these exquisite birds. Once hemlock became a part of the composition, the amount of detail rose exponentially. When there is so much detail involved, the trick is to make sure that I am controlling it, rather than letting it control me. The key lies in being sure every bit of detail included is intentional and serving a purpose rather than simply added for the sake of more.

BERING SEA PIRATES

Parasitic Jaegers & Arctic Tern

Swift and agile beyond belief

In 1986 the Leigh Yawkey Woodson Art Museum asked me to submit a proposal for a major piece. I was given complete freedom with regard to subject matter and encouraged to think big. For years, I had been contemplating a large work involving jaegers—bold and dramatic predators from the far north and the open sea. Here was my opportunity. I submitted a proposal involving three birds in flight: two Parasitic Jaegers pursuing an Arctic Tern. *Jaeger* is a German word that means "hunter." Jaegers take the place of hawks and owls out on the world's oceans. Parasitic Jaegers are pirates that raid and plunder wherever the opportunity presents itself, capable of catching their own prey but more than willing to steal it from another bird if given half a chance. It was this aspect of the bird's behavior that struck me as having powerful sculptural potential. A line from Richard Pough's *Audubon Water Bird Guide* speaks of the drama I wanted to capture: "Swift and agile beyond belief, the parasitic jaeger follows every twist and plunge of the tern until the desperate bird gives up its prey, which the jaeger catches before it hits the water."

My proposal was accepted. Armed with my sketchbook, I headed to Alaska to study the birds that were going to occupy so much of my time for the next several years.

By any measure, *Bering Sea Pirates* is the largest piece that I've done. The tight, detailed nature of my work pulls the viewer in close. The size of *Bering Sea Pirates* requires the viewer to step back in order to take it in as a whole. Comfortable viewing distance is such that the intimate treatment of surface detail is almost lost. Almost. I would do a piece as big as this again (in fact, I have a couple of ideas. . .), but at the time it didn't make sense to me to go any bigger, and it still doesn't. If the viewer is forced to take even one single step farther back, it would be enough to take the intimacy of my work out of range. The manner in which I handle detail and surfaces would become irrelevant.

I'm reminded of a question I asked myself long ago: Would I rather live up high *with* a view or down low *in* the view? I've made my choice. My home and studio are down low, along a stream in a close, intimate setting. I've lost vistas and big skies, but I've gained immediate access to the things around me. I enjoy direct personal contact with anything I see. A view from the mountaintop can be inspirational, but what you are seeing is distant, out of reach, and, to me, somehow less accessible.

Artistically, *Bering Sea Pirates* offers the best of both views. It is big enough to be grand, but not so big as to lose a sense of detail and intimacy.

Before I went to Alaska I had a very different composition in mind than the one that you see here. I had envisioned a rough-and-tumble chariot race—three birds weaving in and out, the two jaegers jockeying for position, each shouldering the other aside and fighting for a clear shot at the tern. Perhaps the lead jaeger would be struggling to get back on track after having missed the tern on its first pass. The second jaeger could be sidestepping over and around the first to bear down on the frantic tern with might and menace.

It all seemed very dramatic in my mind, but it was all wrong. In Alaska, I learned that the birds simply did not do what I had in mind. The jaegers I saw, including young birds, were such skilled and consummate fliers that they simply never got out of step. They were indeed "swift and agile beyond belief" and seemed able to anticipate and match any tactic or maneuver that their quarry would, or could, employ.

I had imagined a brawl—what I saw was a ballet. The power of the drama came from grace and speed rather than muscle.

This new insight led to a significant and fundamental change in the design of the piece. Instead of weaving in and out and braiding together, the birds fell into formation.

I found that the birds appeared faster when they were flying in formation. Every time I had tried to increase action with a twist or a dodge, I had lost speed. Anything that increased speed was a welcome development, and I gladly embraced the new arrangement. The change was a direct result of my fieldwork and shows why it was so important for me to have gone to Alaska.

The sub-adult plumages of jaegers are distinct and attractive. In the "before Alaska" version, I had considered making the struggling jaeger a young bird. Immature plumage could explain his error and at the same time avoid the potential monotony of having two identically patterned birds in the piece.

But when I shifted the birds into formation, I dropped the idea of having one of the jaegers in juvenile plumage. Once behavior due to a young bird's inexperience was eliminated, the reason for including immature plumage seemed to be eliminated as well. Also, I came to realize that all three birds looking distinctly different would fragment the piece. Matching jaegers read more clearly as a two-on-one situation in which the tern was more easily seen as the pursued. The idea that the two jaegers were chasing the tern was strongest when the jaegers were wearing the same uniform.

The trailing jaeger is flying with outstretched wings and a fully spread tail. Its bill is open wide, and its legs and feet dangle out and away from its body. A step ahead, the lead jaeger rushes on with trimmed sails—wings and tail half-closed, bill slightly parted, legs and feet held close. Out in front and moving with all possible speed, the tern rockets ahead, its swept-back wings drawn in, tail closed, bill shut, and feet completely tucked. As each successive bird pulls itself in more tightly, a compositional funnel is created in which the speed builds as the action in the piece narrows and rushes forward. The tern's tight pose and forward position work together to maximize the concept of speed. Its sharply pointed, bright-red bill provides the focal point that leads the entire composition.

I ran the tern right out of the piece. It has no base underneath it. Typically in sculpture, balance is achieved by centering the subject over its base. By placing the tern ahead of the base with its only point of contact a trailing wingtip, I intentionally created an imbalance that I felt would translate into speed—as if the tern's haste could not be contained and has already taken it beyond its confines.

Bering Sea Pirates
40 x 60 x 30
acrylic on basswood and tupelo
1989

The biggest challenge in a piece often comes from elements other than the birds. This was especially true with *Bering Sea Pirates*. I had decided to carve the birds' ocean wave out of stone. Steatite, or soapstone, seemed to have all the qualities I was looking for. A long search, with dead ends from the Arctic Circle to Brazil, led me to an abandoned quarry operation in Virginia, where I found the color, pattern, and most importantly, the size of stone I needed.

With help, I found a large stone I liked and split out the section I wanted. The stone sat outside my studio for a year while I continued working on the jaegers and tern. I studied it often to determine the best way to take advantage of its grain and pattern.

The first thing to do was get the bottom of the stone flat. I flipped it upside-down onto a low dolly. I attached a leg to each corner of an angle iron triangle just big enough to fit around the stone. By adjusting the height of the legs, I could superimpose the plane defined by the triangle onto the stone. Two more pieces of angle iron were used to make a tool guide that could be positioned across two sides of the triangle. I rigged a circular saw to slide across the guide and began to score the stone. High spots were chipped away by hand. The triangle was then lowered and the process repeated until the entire surface was flat.

Top: Soapstone near Schuyler, Virginia
Middle: Splitting my stone by hand
Upper left: Angle iron triangle
Upper right: Triangle with legs and tool guide
Bottom left: Scoring high spots
Bottom right: Chipping away waste

The bottom of the stone was flat but covered with marks left by the saw and chisel. I replaced the saw with a router and milled the rough surface completely smooth. Once the bottom of the stone was finished, I could trim away some bulk by cutting its edges closer to the outline I wanted.

With the stone reduced to a size and weight I could manage, but not so delicate that I had to worry about cracking it, I flipped it onto a heavily reinforced worktable.

Finally, the stone was right-side-up, and I could begin roughing out the shape of the wave. In the beginning, I continued to use a circular saw, mallet, and chisels to quickly remove large amounts of material. As the shape of the wave became more and more refined, its edges got thinner and increasingly more delicate. I switched from the mallet and chisels to an angle grinder with a cutting wheel the size and shape of half a bagel.

The wings were fitted with metal components to support the flying birds. Slots were carefully cut through the stone to receive the brass tabs that were a part of the metal support structure that served to keep the birds aloft.

The wave's final finish was achieved with a combination of sanding, rubbing, buffing, polishing, and burnishing.

Top: The flattened stone flipped onto work table
Upper middle: Roughing out with mallet and chisel
Lower middle: Grinding the wave to final shape
Bottom: The finished wave, buffed and polished

While I worked on *Bering Sea Pirates*, I became increasingly aware of the difference between real motion and speed, evident in the flight of an actual bird, and the illusion of motion and speed I was trying to imply with wood. Real birds actually move. Wooden ones, regardless of pose, do not. If I portray a bird in a motionless pose, resting quietly or sleeping, and do it well enough, it can require close scrutiny to determine whether the object is a carving or a real bird. But a bird in action, especially one presented in flight, no matter how skillfully done, immediately exposes itself as a fake by the very fact that it is stationary. The more animated the pose, the greater the discrepancy.

Bering Sea Pirates was one of the most animated compositions I had ever attempted. I began looking for ways to soften the contrast between the motion and speed I was trying to convey and the static form in which it would be presented. I used the wing positions of the three birds to introduce a subtle hint of animation into the composition. I began to think of each bird as a single frame in a very short film clip. When the frames are put together, the sequence creates a "motion picture" of sorts. The trailing jaeger's wings are up, the middle bird's wings are level, and the tern's wings are down. Collectively, the three birds represent a wingbeat moving through the piece. You get a fuller sense of the actions of any one of the individual birds when you look at all three birds together. Each bird's immediate past and future moments are represented in the other two. A sense of before, during, and after can create a stronger sense of movement than a frozen instant.

The last issue in the design of *Bering Sea Pirates* was the question of whether or not to put a fish in the tern's bill. Leaving the fish out could open the piece up to a misinterpretation of the jaegers' intentions. They are not necessarily after the tern itself—they are after the fish it just caught. From an ornithological perspective, accuracy would probably dictate that a fish would be held crosswise in the tern's bill, but that would interfere with the lines of the piece artistically. The tern's bright-red bill is the strongest bit of color in the entire piece, and it had taken on a significant role in the composition. I wanted to keep the area clean and simple. This was a dilemma for me. Accuracy and field study have always been important to me, but I had strong ideas about what I wanted artistically.

I had a chance to talk about the matter with Don Eckelberry, an artist I respect tremendously who has written eloquently about the concerns and issues that involve birds, art, and illustration. His work has been a major influence on mine. I hoped his insight would

somehow make my decision easier. To what extent could I disregard scientific concerns in lieu of artistic ones? Could I get away with leaving the fish out? Would it be missed? He thought it would be clearer and do a better job of storytelling if the fish were included. But noting my artistic concerns, he thought for a moment and then resolved my dilemma beautifully, especially in light of the title of the piece, when he said, "Well, I guess when the pirate ship is chasing the merchant vessel, they don't necessarily have the gold stacked on the deck." That clinched it for me, and the fish disappeared "down the hatch."

It was extremely fitting and pleasing to me that Don Eckelberry could be a part of the last chapter of *Bering Sea Pirates'* story, for he was there at the very beginning as well: the field guide with Richard Pough's description that had fired my imagination was illustrated by none other than Don Eckelberry. It was his guide I had grown up with. And it was *his* illustrations of jaegers that had inspired me to do mine.

A fish in the tern's bill favors science—leaving it out favors art. Sometimes art and science are allies; sometimes they are not. In my work, I try to strike a balance between the two. I look for solutions that satisfy both. In this case, the concept that is most important to me is the idea of the chase. Whether the viewer thinks the jaegers are after the tern itself or the fish the tern has swallowed, the piece still reads as a pursuit.

VANTAGE POINT

Loggerhead Shrike & Hawthorn

The role of detail

Our eyes are naturally drawn to detail. Looking up into the vastness of the night sky, we seek out the clusters of stars that form the constellations. Looking down at our feet, we disregard the featureless sidewalk but take note of the cracks. In almost any situation, our eyes move toward the area of greatest detail. We kneel down to admire the complexity of a spider's web or to study the intricate structure of a tiny flower. We look for detail, and when we find it we look even harder. Our measure of how well we have seen something is determined by the amount of detail we can recall. Our attraction to detail is a constant force, like gravity, invisible and powerful, relentlessly pulling us in.

Detail plays a prominent role in my work. It is important, but not what is *most* important. Detail tends to focus attention on parts. I focus on the integrated whole, which is of greater concern to me than the techniques used to bring the piece into being. My goal, as a sculptor, is to create a whole that is greater than its constituent parts. With bird carving, I find it's easy to get lost in detail. The key to keeping detail from taking over is to use it thoughtfully and intentionally,

when and where it is needed and supports the main idea. I think of it as a vehicle that can help me get where I want to go, but is not the destination itself.

Detail, and the techniques and skills used to create it, makes up the vocabulary of bird carving. A good vocabulary provides us with the words we need to express ourselves, but the words themselves are not enough. Words cannot express coherent thoughts until they are put together in meaningful ways and arranged into articulate sentences. Those sentences assembled in logical ways combine and grow in number until a story is told. Without words, the entire endeavor never gets off the ground, but once the story is told, it becomes more important than the individual words used to tell it.

It's the same with my sculpture. Detail and technique have inherent value but need to be put together in coherent, intentional ways to tell a good visual story. In *Vantage Point*, I began to think about using detail more judiciously than I previously had. I started to place the detail precisely where it needed to be in order to create movement to direct the viewer's eye where I wanted it to go.

Vantage Point
26 x 10 x 11
acrylic on basswood
1991

I have been watching birds my whole life. I've spent hours and hours looking for them, tracking them down, spotting them, bringing up the binoculars and adjusting the focus all in one smooth motion, and then being transfixed by the beauty and detail revealed through the lens. Binoculars concentrate our attention. They intensify the act of observation by magnifying the subject, while at the same time blacking out everything beyond a limited field of view. They provide an extremely powerful way of seeing. It makes sense that something from that method of observation would creep into my sculptural imagery.

Vantage Point's clean black base has no detail. There is nothing to hold your eye. Its bold simplicity is so easily and immediately understood that it is dismissed. In a photograph of the entire piece, the black base is hard to miss, but in person you look past it as if it weren't even there. The metal branch carries enough detail to make it clearly identifiable as hawthorn, but not enough detail to keep your eye from moving on to the area of greatest detail: the bird itself.

In a way, *Vantage Point* is a sculptural version of bird watching, the equivalent of seeing a bird in the field through binoculars. I've used detail to center all focus and attention on the bird itself. You are aware of the branch, but only peripherally. Anything and everything beyond the branch is eliminated and falls away.

Shrikes are songbirds, but they act like birds of prey. They capture and kill with their strong, hooked beaks, but their songbird feet lack the strength to grasp and render their prey. Shrikes often hang or impale their victims on thorns to secure them while they are being torn apart, or to cache them for later use. This habit has earned them the nickname of "butcher bird."

I knew from the start that I would place my shrike in hawthorn. I returned to the studio with some freshly cut hawthorn, along with a few wounds acquired while collecting the thorny branches. As I considered the branches, it occurred to me that I already held in my hands a real branch that I was going to use as a model to make another one just like it, which I would then use in my sculpture. In other words, I was going to spend the next month or so working to get back to where I already was. I also had been thinking about the inherent nature of the materials I use. Paint covers and eliminates any chance for the materials to contribute to the piece. I use wood and metal but they never show.

The "butcher bird" and the well-armed hawthorn are both cold and ruthless, each in its own way. I chose to leave my hawthorn branch unpainted. The cold, bare metal and the brightly polished, gleaming thorns seem to echo the character of both the shrike and the hawthorn. The bare metal branch conveys something about the personality of each in a way that a more literal, realistic branch could not. The polished brass also adds a touch of color that enhances and enlivens an otherwise neutral composition.

Representational art doesn't need to be limited
to photo-realistic duplication. While working on
Vantage Point, I began to think of nature—and
realism—as a starting point rather than the goal.

In the Cattails

Least Bittern & Marsh Wren

Near and far afield

In the spring of 1992, I took part in a field expedition organized by the Artists for Nature Foundation (ANF). I was one of thirty-two artists from fifteen countries who traveled to the vast wetlands that lie along the Biebrza and Narew Rivers in northeast Poland. We lived and worked for two weeks on the edges of one of the last remaining lowland marshes in Europe.

ANF works with artists to bring attention to areas that are under threat and in need of conservation. The premise is a simple one. Many people see little worth in what they perceive to be a wasteland. ANF brings in artists who find and respond to the inherent beauty of the region. Their artwork seen in exhibitions and books draws attention to the concerns of the district and inspires and influences those in whose hands the future lies. Often people will respond more readily to the artwork than they will to the place, object, or thing that inspired it. Art can open people's eyes to value and beauty that was previously hidden to them.

I feel a kinship with ANF's philosophy in part because it is so similar to my own. My work is an invitation to look a little closer, an encouragement to pause and consider the subtle beauty of things that often go unnoticed, to dwell for a moment on the little things that, in the end, are often the most important.

The common denominator of all the artists on the ANF project was the ability to work in the field. I relate to this as well because of the importance and reliance that I place on fieldwork. My sketchbooks are the very basis and foundation of my work. Almost all of my pieces can be traced back to an experience in the field. The pages of my sketchbooks stand as a record and reminder of the encounters I've had and the things I've seen. My sketchbooks are the most valuable and powerful resource in my studio. They contain far more information than just what is recorded on their pages. The act of sketching is often more important than the sketch itself, because sketching is really about seeing. Observation is the main event. The sketch is simply a record of that observation. Often the relationship I am able to forge with a subject during the process of making the sketch, even if the time is very brief, is of greater value to me than the sketch itself. My sketches trigger my memories of those connections and all the details and recollections associated with them. There is information contained in my sketches that is available only to me and can be more meaningful than the marks and drawings on the page. A good sketch is the result of having spent the time to see something well. Careful observation is the starting point of everything I do.

In the Cattails
36 x 16 x 22
acrylic on tupelo
1993

59

Little Bittern
field sketch
Biebrza River Basin, Poland
May 12, 1992

One of the birds I saw in Poland was a Little Bittern, *Ixobrychus minutus*. The bird flushed out of the vegetation with a few loose wingbeats, dangled briefly, and dropped back down out of sight. I didn't get as long a look as I would have liked—one rarely does with bitterns—but I saw enough to make a few quick sketches on the spot. I'm quite fond of bitterns and considered the sighting one of the highlights of the trip. Their inconspicuous manner and secretive ways make opportunities to see them all too infrequent.

A few days after returning home from Poland, I got a much closer look at another bittern. I received a call from Powdermill, the bird banding station near my home, to let me know they had just captured a Least Bittern, *Ixobrychus exilis*, the North American counterpart to the bittern I had just seen in the Biebrza marshes a continent away. It was the banding station's first Least Bittern in almost thirty years. I was there within minutes with my sketchbook.

Following up on the brief encounter I'd had in Europe with the intimate opportunity to actually handle a Least Bittern and examine it closely was a marvelous bit of good fortune. There was no need to choose between a bird in the hand and a bird in the bush—I'd had one of each!

Least Bittern
drawn from a handheld bird
Powdermill Nature Reserve
June 4, 1992

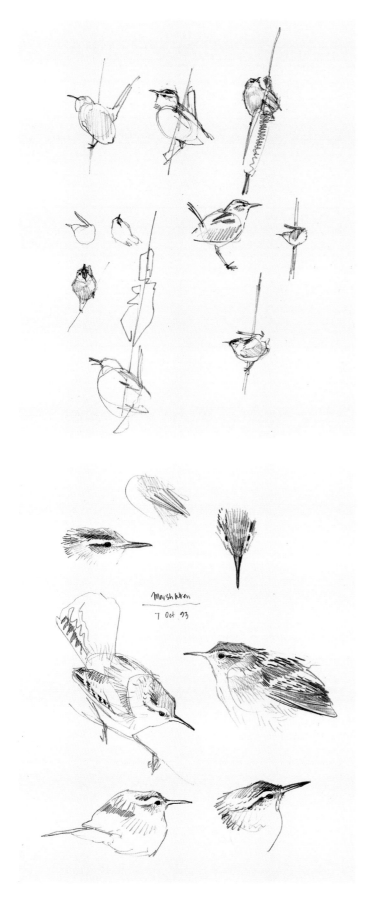

Marsh Wren
field sketch
Nisqually National Wildlife Refuge, Washington
June 13, 1992

Two weeks later I was traveling on the West Coast. I visited the Nisqually National Wildlife Refuge, just southwest of Seattle, Washington, where I spent some time in a large cattail marsh. The cattails were teeming with Marsh Wrens. A boardwalk path allowed me to get into the midst of the birds, which were singing enthusiastically from the tops of cattail heads all around me. Sketching birds in the field is not usually so easy, but the birds were so accessible it was almost like sketching handheld birds back home at Powdermill. And just as with the bitterns, it was not long before I did, in fact, have a Marsh Wren in my hand at Powdermill.

At the time I made these sketches, I had no plans to carve a bittern or a wren. I was simply paying attention to the things that were around me and sketching to record what I was seeing.

Later in the year, with no strong ideas about what I would be carving next, I visited Carnegie Museum's Section of Birds and browsed through the study skin collection, hoping to find the inspiration for my next piece. I borrowed half a dozen different skins of birds that interested me. It wasn't until I was home that I realized two of the skins I had selected, a bittern and a Marsh Wren, could work well together in one piece. Looking back through my sketchbooks, I found the bitterns and wrens on adjacent pages, as if I'd been planning the two together the whole time.

Marsh Wren
drawn from a handheld bird
Powdermill Nature Reserve
October 7, 1993

61

In its simplest terms, the design of *In the Cattails* consists of two separate but equal elements located at opposite ends of a strong diagonal. The two birds are the opposing elements I needed to bring into balance. Least Bitterns are not very big, but they are a lot bigger than Marsh Wrens. There is a tendency for the larger bird in a composition to be seen as the dominant bird. With *In the Cattails*, I wanted the two birds to be seen as equal partners in the composition despite their difference in size. I did not want the smaller wren to be seen as a token extra. Though the wren is a smaller bird, I wanted it to carry the same visual weight as the larger bittern.

In order to elevate its stature and importance, I placed the wren high, at the very top of the composition. And rather than perching it on the stem above or below the cattail head, I placed the wren directly on the bulky head. Joined together, the bird and the cattail head present a mass closer to that of the bittern below.

I opted to present the wren energetically engaged in song. The singing wrens I had seen and sketched in the Nisqually marsh had shown me how much impact a small bird could have. The energy projected by a singing bird can make the bird seem bigger than it really is. The high placement of the wren, combined with its energy, enable the tiny wren to hold its own in a composition with a much larger bird.

Bitterns are long-necked, long-legged, long-billed wading birds that favor marshes and wetlands. They are closely related to the herons and egrets with whom they share the same physical characteristics. Herons and egrets are far better known, in large part because their feeding habits require them to spend much of their time standing out in the open in places where they are easy to notice. Bitterns take a different approach. They are skulkers that stay hidden in the dense vegetation of a wetland among the grasses, reeds, and cattails. They work from cover rather than out in the open.

Bitterns have an unusual and curious way of dealing with a threat heading their way. In an effort to avoid detection, they routinely freeze with their bills pointed skyward and face the threat head-on, enabling the tawny streaking that runs down their neck to blend with their surroundings remarkably well. Bitterns have even been known to deliberately sway to keep time with the movement of the cattails in a breeze. Their habits are so ingrained that they can be approached quite closely while convinced they are invisible.

An added benefit of placing the wren so high in the composition was that it allows the iconic pose of the bittern to make more sense to those who are unfamiliar with the habits of these secretive birds. If you don't know about this characteristic behavior, you might wonder why the bittern has its bill pointing straight up. When we come across a man on the street or sidewalk looking straight up, we don't continue to look at him—we follow his gaze. We ask what he's looking at, what's up there. The wren brings an end to any questions about why the bittern is looking up or what it is looking at. I used it to help the bittern's habit work, which in turn made the whole piece work. The wren's presence gives the bittern a reason to be looking up. The bittern doesn't need the reason, but to a viewer who doesn't know anything about bitterns, it softens the strangeness of the habit that might seem peculiar otherwise.

Scientific accuracy is important to me, but so is pure sculptural form. My work is a blend of both. I happen to like birds, so I choose to feature them in my work. But I am just as interested in working with the basic principles of art and design, which apply regardless of subject matter. Sculptural concepts that can be understood in pure, abstract terms are just as much a part of my work as a working knowledge of avian anatomy and feather tracts. The decisions I make while working out designs and compositions are guided by the concerns of both art and science. I am uncomfortable with a sculptural solution that only works if the viewer knows what I know about birds and their habits. I enjoy finding ways to work out the concerns of art and science simultaneously. It pleases me when a solution presents itself from one side and helps solve a problem from the other, like when a purely abstract need for more volume or mass helps me decide where to place a wren on a cattail.

It's my choice to do birds, but a piece needs to work first and foremost as sculpture with the surface detail stripped away. Underneath a façade that is faithful to natural history and science, there must be an abstract sculptural foundation.

GREAT REED WARBLER

Acrocephalus arundinaceus

Outside sources of inspiration

Do I place the bird high or low in the composition? How far should I turn the head and in what direction? Should I raise the wings over the tail or drop them below it? If the wingtips are crossed, will the right or the left side be on top? Should the breast feathers overlap the wing and cover it fully, or partially, or will the wrist be exposed? Will the tail be spread or remain closed? Should the individual tail feathers be compressed together tightly, or held more loosely and show some separation? How high should the crest be raised? How many feather splits should I include, and where should those splits be placed?

Every decision matters. Each one is affected by the decisions made around it, and together they all contribute to and become part of an orchestrated whole. The attitude of the bird, its countenance and character, and the sense of life it projects are determined by the constant, continuous string of intentional decisions I make day in and day out while working in the studio. However, I find that the most important decisions, the moments of real epiphany, often occur while I am out of the studio.

When my hands are engaged, my attention is automatically focused on the business at hand: the execution of technical skills. It is when I lay down my tools, leave the studio, and temporarily disengage myself from the tasks that require such concentration that my mind can entertain the questions of *what* to do rather than *how* to do it.

The real moments of clarity—when thoughts crystallize and a piece comes together—occur when I am removed, at least to some degree, from the piece, rather than working on it directly. It is while I'm cutting firewood, out in the canoe, or driving to town—when my mind is engaged with the work but my hands are free of it—that my random thoughts (which aren't really random after all) are free to float and drift, merge, align, and connect with each other in new and unexpected ways. The short walk from the house back to the studio can become a long one. I may need to see if the orchids are blooming, or if the morels are up, or check on the trout in the upper pool—not because any of these things need my attention, but because I need the gentle distraction they provide. I need to step away. I need time to think.

Great Reed Warbler
40 x 8 x 8
acrylic on basswood
1997

Great Reed Warbler
field sketch (shown actual size)
Narew River, Waniewo, Poland
May 24, 1992

The next-to-last morning during my time in Poland with ANF, we headed out into the fens in punts. It was a still morning, but not a quiet one. A healthy marsh in spring is filled with the voices of the many birds that live there. A Great Reed Warbler suddenly appeared in the open, perched high on a single bare reed. It was a powerful image. I made a quick sketch of the bird and his linear perch—not elaborate or detailed, but enough to remember. The sketch still triggers memories I have of that morning: the damp chill, the harsh mix of sounds, the surge of the punt with the pole, and the rich color of the bird against a sky of white mist.

I carried the image in my mind for the next several years, very open to the idea of presenting it sculpturally. *Great Reed Warbler* is a synthesis of a number of ideas, influences, and solutions that I came across during those years that reinforced, affected, and modified my thinking and, ultimately, led to the design of my piece.

The exhibition "Natural Wonders," a collection of work honoring Alice and John Forester of the Leigh Yawkey Woodson Art Museum, included a painting of aspen leaves by Heather Dieter Bartmann. It was a lovely, delicate watercolor, but it was the simple, clean, and elegant way it was presented that caught my eye. Rich, rusty hues, warm whites, and golden accents blended together seamlessly. What lingered in my mind afterward was the way the perfectly proportioned mat and frame enhanced the simple image and made it even better.

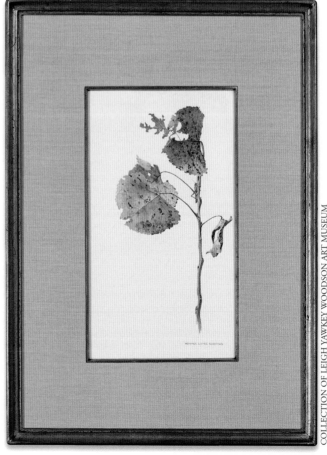

Heather Dieter Bartmann's
Last Fling
acrylic on ragboard
16 x 8^1/$_2$
1992

Blyth's Reed Warbler

1st-winter

Marsh Warbler

1st-winter

Reed Warbler

Lars Jonsson's *Acrocephalus*
warblers illustration in *Birds of Europe with
North Africa and the Middle East*
1993

Not long after my time in Poland, Lars Jonsson's *Birds of Europe with North Africa and the Middle East* was published. The guide is filled with hundreds of plates and illustrations that are as artistically satisfying, to my eye, as any I have seen. One of the illustrations of *Acrocephalus* Warblers (closely related to the Great Reed Warbler) was particularly attractive. Like Bartmann's painting, the birds are a combination of warm whites and rich golden browns, pleasing shapes perched on simple, straight stems. Seeing the warbler plate increased my desire to sculpt the bird I had seen in Poland.

Later, on a visit to the Met, I came away thinking more about the display of the objects I'd seen than about the objects themselves. On that particular visit, I had been interested in seeing the patinas on bronze artifacts. The artifacts were beautifully displayed on thick brass plates. Always on the lookout for successful design solutions, I took note of the clean and simple presentation of the richly colored objects. The solution was elegant and effective.

In a private home, I saw another frame that caught my eye: a commissioned portrait, very well done and very well framed, included a beautifully engraved brass nameplate. I am not a fan of brass plaques. Most seem to do more harm than good, but this one worked. The brass plate was thick. The engraving was deep, cut by hand rather than machine. It was a touch of elegant detail that made both the frame and the painting better.

Great Reed Warbler
detail of engraved base
1997

71

This piece appears to be very simple, but it was actually quite challenging and taxed my understanding of anatomy more than usual. While I am working in clay, I frequently adopt the pose of the bird I am sculpting in an effort to better understand it. Mindful of the likenesses and differences in our anatomies, I perch on a stool or table, imagining that I am the bird—all the while hoping no visitors happen to drop by. I may look silly crouched on my tiptoes with my arms folded or flapping, but it helps. It provides insight that can determine which way I turn a head, whether to drop a shoulder, or how to cross the primaries. I tried this exercise with the Great Reed Warbler and found it was not as helpful as usual because I simply could not assume the position of the bird. I could not cling to a vertical pole with my feet.

Great Reed Warblers live in a world of vertical reeds. They contort and twist their bodies into extreme positions all day long, and yet they look totally at ease in these strained positions. I wanted to do the same thing the real birds do: make a complex and difficult pose look easy. In order for my carving of a Great Reed Warbler to be convincing, it would have to appear to be as comfortable as the real bird.

I work hard to make what I do look easy. If I do my job well, then the viewer's attention is focused on the bird rather than on me and my efforts. I want everything about the piece to look easy, casual, and nonchalant, even if not one single part of making it was. I want the bird to look relaxed, totally comfortable with itself and its surroundings. I want the elements of the composition to be arranged in such a way that they don't appear to have been arranged at all.

Even though each element has been carefully considered, I want everything to look as though it has simply fallen into place on its own, without any help from me. I want my birds to appear graceful and effortless because that is how the real birds look to me. They appear out of nowhere, glorious, stunning, beautiful forms that blend perfectly with the landscape and, at the same time, stand out apart from it. And then, just as quickly, they are gone. Afterward, I always feel fortunate to have had a short, brief glimpse into their world.

I strive to make the work seem as effortless as possible so that all that stands before you is the simple, clean beauty of the bird itself.

GREEN HERON

Butorides virescens

"Self expression calls attention to the self, art to the thing made." —Aidan Chambers

I was once asked what I am trying to say with my work. I think I surprised the interviewer—and myself—when I responded instantly with, "Nothing. Absolutely nothing." I went on to explain that the idea of saying something seemed backward to me. My work had always been the result of my listening rather than talking. My focus is on hearing and seeing what Nature has to say, rather than on what I have to say. My work has always been my response to the beauty I see in the natural world. I struggle to internalize that beauty, to bring it under control, to somehow take possession of it, and to instill it in my work, all in an effort to do it justice. The struggle is a personal one. It is between me and Art, with very little room for outside concerns. While I am in the midst of the effort, my energy is devoted to resolving and reconciling the issues in play—to better understanding beauty, art, and how the two fit together. The last thing on my mind is what I am trying to say.

But the question got me thinking once again about what I do and why I do it. Just how would I define it? Some might assume that my goal is to duplicate nature, to trick the viewer into thinking what I have made is "real." I think this assumption has more to do with the fact that the work is three-dimensional than it does

with the high degree of realism involved. No one looks at a painting of a landscape, no matter how realistically it has been done, and thinks that it might actually be the real thing. It's clearly a painting.

No doubt there is a strong component of realism in my work, but it is not my intention to trick the viewer into thinking that what I have made is real any more than a landscape painter wants you to think that the trees he has painted on canvas are actually real trees. People will say they *look* real, but they are not likely to confuse them with the real ones. They always know the painting is a painting. If it is extremely realistic, they might say it looks like a photograph, but even photographs are still understood to be representations of the object depicted.

But when the realistic object before them is three-dimensional *and* actual size, it is understandable why some might mistakenly think my goal is to duplicate nature. It is not—it just looks that way. Making the piece as realistically as I do is my way of exploring and internalizing what it is about that object (bird, plant, rock, etc.) that appeals to me. The finished piece represents what I have learned about the beauty of one small piece of the world around us—a beauty I have come to know and would like others to know too.

Green Heron
6 x 14 x 4
acrylic on tupelo
1999

As I try to identify just what it is that compels me, I get caught up in questions. What is attractive to me and why? What is beauty? What are the qualities and attributes that create it? My ongoing struggle to identify and answer these questions is what keeps me in the game, looking, questioning, and thinking. Yes, my work is highly representational, and I welcome the response that it looks real, but that isn't my goal.

I use realism to better understand what I have seen and felt moved by, and then to high-light and bring attention to that beauty. With birds, the beauty is often ethereal, there for a moment and then gone. I linger. I hold on to that image. I study it. I explore it. I immerse myself in it. My work is the result of the time I spend with it. But I take on the task in the spirit of reverence, rather than competition. No matter how realistic my efforts, they fall far short of the beauty of that which motivates me. My hope is that I can trigger the same response in the viewer. If the viewer reacts to my work in a way similar to how I reacted to the real bird, then my efforts to capture that imagery have been to some degree successful.

It's easy to think of a bird as being defined by its feathers. But it is the parts that are not feathered—the eyes, bill, and feet—that carry the attitude of the bird.

In my sculpture, I find I can take quite a few liberties with the feathers, but the eyes, bills, and feet require a much tighter discipline. The feathers that cloak a bird's body don't reveal a bird's soul any more than the clothes we wear define us. If we want to really get to know someone, we must meet them face to face and look into their eyes. I feel the same way about birds. The shapes of their eyes are particularly expressive. They can convey alert intensity or a calm sense of ease with the slightest nuance, just as ours can. A bill raised or lowered by a single degree can completely change the look of the entire bird. A bird's feet are similar to our hands; their rear-facing hind toe functions in much the same way as our thumbs, enabling birds to grasp objects just as we do. The feet are as expressive as our hands and, together with the legs, determine the stance and gesture that convince us the bird is in motion or at rest.

Though they represent a small percentage of a bird's surface area, the eyes, bills, legs, and feet do most of the work in determining a bird's attitude, personality, and character.

A Green Heron is an ideal bird to be presented in such a simple, straightforward manner. My carved heron stands alone, without so much as a single blade of grass to accompany it. The bird itself becomes the composition. I felt a heron, with its large feet and interesting shape, could hold up to the scrutiny it would receive in a composition consisting of the bird and nothing more.

The bird's habits work well with a presentation that relies so heavily on the viewer's imagination. Green Herons are seldom seen far from water. Any flat surface my carved heron is set upon can easily be seen as the smooth surface of a quiet, shallow pool or a mudflat along the water's edge. The small herons stalk their prey with slow and steady movements, frequently pausing in mid-stride. The real birds' habit of freezing and remaining motionless for long periods of time makes my immobile carved heron all the more believable.

I felt the concept of the piece was stronger with the bird in immature plumage. The young heron is more heavily patterned and streaked than the more formally attired adult. In a composition that is so casually presented, without a formal base, it seemed appropriate to keep the dress code casual as well.

A good base can be an important component of a successful sculpture, but it also provides the first clue that the bird is not real. I've spent a lot of time outdoors looking at birds, and I've never seen one on a hand-rubbed walnut base. To make this heron seem as real as possible, I left out everything that would suggest otherwise. He is simply there, just as a real bird would be.

TIDAL COMPANIONS

Ruddy Turnstone & Purple Sandpipers

"How long did that take?"

The question I am asked more frequently than any other is always a variation of "How long did that take?" Versions of my short, off-the-cuff answers include: I don't know. I have no idea. I don't keep track. I don't even *want* to know. I just work on them until they are finished—however long that takes doesn't really matter. The clock doesn't have anything to do with it. While all of these responses are true, they aren't very helpful, and none of them actually answers the question.

The question is a fair one, and I'd like to answer it, but I can't without knowing two things: when I started and when I finished. I usually know exactly when I finished a piece, but I can rarely say with the same degree of certainty when the work began.

It's a lot like the seasonal movement of birds, but in reverse. It's easy to note the arrival date of the year's first phoebe, but it's much harder to note the day that they depart. The first phoebe of the year is met with joy and celebration, but the last phoebe quietly slips away unnoticed. And then one day you realize that it's been awhile since you've seen one and they might already be gone. Without records, there is no way to pin down the date the bird was last seen. With my

sculpture, the starting points are often as vague as the first day that I *didn't* see the phoebes anymore.

Records are the key, and I don't usually have them. Ideas that come together gradually, over time, don't usually have clearly identifiable points of origin—at least, not in the form of a time or a date. *Tidal Companions*, however, is a grand exception. Not only do I have a clear starting point for *Tidal Companions*, I also have a specific date to go with that starting point, and enough additional material for me to be able to trace the piece from beginning to end. It is highly unusual for me to have this amount of documentation on a piece that has spent so much of its time as nothing more than an idea. With the following time-line that tracks *Tidal Companions* from start to finish, I hope to give you a sense of how a piece comes together, how it evolves, and how it develops over time; and, finally, to provide a more thorough answer to the question, "How long did that take?"

Not every piece I do has a story as long as *Tidal Companions'*, but the process you see here is representative of my approach to sculpture. In my experience, figuring out *what* to do has always been more difficult and more time consuming than the actual doing.

Tidal Companions
12 x 12 x 10
acrylic on tupelo
2000

A TIMELINE

APRIL 26th 1976

D.CR CORMORANT	SANDERLING
GREAT BLUE HERON	RUDDY TURNSTONE
SNOWY EGRET	PURPLE SANDPIPER
LOUISIANA HERON	WILLET
GREEN HERON	HERRING GULL
GLOSSY IBIS	RING BILLED GULL
MALLARD	LAUGHING GULL
WOOD DUCK	CASPIAN TERN
REDHEAD	ROCK DOVE
RED BR MERGANSER	MOURNING DOVE
TURKEY VULTURE	CHIMNEY SWIFT
RED TAILED HAWK	YELLOW SH. FLICKER
BOB WHITE	BARN SWALLOW
OYSTERCATCHER	BLUE JAY
SEMIPALMATED PLOVER	CROW
KILLDEER	B C CHICKADEE
BLACK BELLIED PLOVER	CAROLINA WREN

In April 1976 I was eighteen and attended the Ward Foundation's World Championship Wildfowl Carving Competition for the first time. No one uses the show's full name. The carvers refer to it as the Ward Show, the Worlds, or simply OC in reference to Ocean City, Maryland, where the event is held annually.

While there, I spent some time exploring the area. I discovered a rocky cove at the south end of town in the lee of the large stone jetty that protected the mouth of the inlet. The small cove was filled with Ruddy Turnstones and Purple Sandpipers, the first I had ever seen. It was my habit at that time to keep lists of all the birds that I saw in a day—especially a day when I was on the road in a new area where I was likely to see new and different birds. I would underline the name of any bird seen for the first time that year. Life birds—those seen for the first time *ever*—received the additional distinction of being recorded in red. I still have the day's list that includes Ruddy Turnstones and Purple Sandpipers, side by side and written in red.

The carving show had quite an impact on me, and so did the new birds I'd seen. I left the show more excited than ever about birds and carving. The idea of carving a mixed flock of shorebirds based on the birds I'd seen in the cove was firmly planted in my mind. It wasn't just the birds—I liked the rocks as well. I saw the rocks as an important part of the composition. Turnstones are somewhat adaptable and can be found in a number of different settings. Purple Sandpipers are far more specialized. They are seldom found far away from rocky shores. A combination of the two species would only be likely if rocks were involved.

Every year while at the Ward Show, I would check in on what I started to think of as "my" birds. They were always there, in the same spot, and my desire to carve them continued to grow stronger and stronger.

Within a few years, I was making serious plans to move ahead with the shorebird piece. I went to Maine in search of the perfect rocky shore. I found it on Mount Desert Island and brought a small piece of it home with me, along with gallon jugs filled with rock-weed and seawater. I also collected boxes and boxes of barnacles, mussels, bits of shell, crab claws, urchins, pebbles, and periwinkles.

Back home, I went to the Carnegie Museum of Natural History in Pittsburgh and continued a discussion about the project with Dr. Kenneth Parkes, the head of the Section of Birds. I had introduced Dr. Parkes to my Ocean City flock shortly after I had found them. He had seen and photographed the coop-erative birds, and had even used one of his photographs of them on his Christmas card. I borrowed study skins from the Section of Birds that covered all stages of plumage and molt for both birds. I was very interested in including one or two of the turnstones in winter plumage, just as I had seen in the Ocean City flock. Using plasticine, I put together a rough but life-size model of what I had in mind. I pictured a dozen birds, maybe even more, crowded close to one another on a high point of rock not yet covered by the rising tide. Quiet birds, active birds, feeding birds, loafing birds—birds sleeping, stretching, and preening—all forced together by a wave washing over their rock festooned with seaweed and encrusted with barnacles.

I suppose we chalk this one up to youthful enthu-siasm. It was a very ambitious project. Unfortunately, it was too ambitious. The piece had become so large and complex that I was never able to take it beyond the clay model, which survives in photographs and a few of the individual clay figures. One by one, and bit by bit, the rest of the clay birds and the clay rocks have been reused, recycled into other birds and other projects.

PHOTO BY ALAN WYCHECK

My plans to carve the entire coast of Maine along with so many birds doing so many things had doomed the project. The shorebird project stalled because of its sheer size and weight. I returned the study skins to the Section of Birds and, over time, disassembled the clay model. Although I never did the piece, I always wanted to. It lived on in my mind as "the best piece I never did."

I maintain two separate series of sketchbooks. My field books, as the name suggests, are the ones that I take into the field. Everything in them has been drawn directly from life. They are a record of what I have *seen*. My studio sketchbooks are quite different. They are a record of what I am *thinking*. The images you see here are representative of the mix of loose doodles and sketches that I put down quickly in my studio sketch-books. It's how I work my way through the thoughts and ideas that come to me. These sketches can be carefully drawn, but usually they are done somewhat absentmindedly with no obvious intent. Their purpose is simply to move ideas from inside of my head out onto paper where I can see them.

Clearly, the shorebird piece was still on my mind. The image surfaced again and again in the casual draw-ings I made as I constantly sifted through thoughts and ideas, both old and new, in an effort to give those ideas form and substance.

1983   1984

PURPLE SANDPIPERS

KILDEER

turnstone

91

HEAD LINES

COVE

mini
headland

B.BEACH

overhang

headshake

tues8m
8:00

Wing stretch
yawn

heads rise as the
weight of the flock rises

92

This composite drawing came off the top of a large sketchpad that served as my desk blotter for a time. Whatever was on my mind made its way onto the page. It is another example of the sort of drawings that can be found in my studio sketchbooks.

Cumulatively, these studio drawings, so often done on whatever scrap of paper was closest at the time, are a fair indication of what I am thinking about and the directions in which I am headed. I have learned to place a certain amount of artistic trust in them. When variations of the same image continue to appear over and over again for five, ten, fifteen years or more, I can't help but conclude that the idea is valid and worthy of continued effort and exploration.

The Ruddy Turnstones and Purple Sandpipers were not going away. The idea was kept alive through drawings and sketches that continued to flow years and years after I thought I had put the project aside.

Turnstones, sandpipers, and others
studio drawing
ballpoint pen and pencil
18 x 24

During the 1990s, I did a number of pieces in which I employed a sort of visual shorthand. I presented a small section of a larger habitat in such a way that the viewer would fill in the rest of the scene.

In the Hardwoods conveys the size, mass, and character of a big tree without overpowering the bird. The clean, clearly defined section of tree allows the viewer to fill in the rest.

Eastern Phoebes presents enough roof for the viewer to be able to place the two birds in context, but not so much roof that the small birds are overpowered by their setting.

Forbesway Drummer presents a ruffed grouse moving along on the top of a fallen log. Once again, enough information is provided for the viewer to imagine the rest of the scene.

In all three of these pieces, I was dealing with settings that could have easily overwhelmed the birds. There are times when I want to do just that—make the piece more about the setting than the bird. But in each of these cases, I wanted the birds to have more emphasis. I wanted the settings to support the birds rather than compete with them.

In the Hardwoods
Pileated Woodpecker
34 x 7 x 7
acrylic on basswood and tupelo
1994

The next time the Ruddy Turnstone and Purple Sandpiper combination resurfaced, I considered the old idea in the light of my new ideas about presentation. There was some potential in the way that my new thoughts could be applied to the shorebird piece—a piece that had always been so big that it never had a chance. Maybe I didn't have to carve the entire coast of Maine after all. Maybe all I needed to do was get the viewer to *think* that I had—to present just enough to get the ball rolling, and then let the viewer take it from there.

It seemed that the shorebird idea had managed to hang around long enough that finally, at long last, a solution had stepped forth to claim it. New thoughts about presentation and design had suddenly brought new life to an old idea.

Top: *Eastern Phoebes*
12 x 9 x 5
acrylic on basswood
1999
Bottom: *Forbesway Drummer*
Ruffed Grouse
17 x 14 x 10
acrylic on basswood
1992

1996

I started to see a change in the studio sketches and conceptual drawings of the shore-bird piece. As I mentioned earlier, my studio drawings are often done almost subconsciously, as if the pencil in my hand were the sensitive, wavering stylus of a lie detector, responding to signals that come from me but are not fully under my conscious control. The drawings are manifestations of my thoughts and emotions and reflect changes and shifts in them.

The piece was changing. Freeform shapes were squaring up. The image was becoming simpler: leaner, tighter, more compact. The piece was developing a new efficiency as the elements within it were reduced and reordered. The old composition was making self-corrections auto-matically as it aligned itself with my new thoughts about design and presentation.

In 1996 I went back again to the same cove in Ocean City where I had first seen Ruddy Turnstones and Purple Sandpipers twenty years earlier. The birds, as consistent as ever, were there as usual, and I sketched them with renewed enthusiasm as I made plans to sculpt a new version of an old idea. I don't know the typical life expectancy for a Ruddy Turnstone or a Purple Sandpiper, but I couldn't help wondering if there were any chance at all that perhaps, just maybe, one of the birds I was sketching was a bird I had seen and sketched before.

The piece I had carried in my mind had been so big for so long that I had a hard time reducing the composition to such a small subset of the original idea. For years, the success of the piece had depended upon including as *much* of the scene as possible. My new goal was to convey all the richness of that same scene, fully and completely, with as *little* as possible.

Top: Ruddy Turnstones, Purple Sandpipers, and Tern field studies
Ocean City, Maryland
Bottom: Purple Sandpiper color study
acrylic on polymer clay
10 x 6 x 6

I started to work on the piece in early January 2000. Things began to move quickly. A new pace and sense of purpose is reflected in the timeline, which now counts by months rather than years. I made a number of clay birds, more than I would include in the new design, but I wanted to give myself some compositional options. I still hadn't found the right combination and continued to experiment with different groupings, placing birds together in different ways and at varying heights, distances, and angles.

I began carving the birds in wood, starting with the ones I felt were most likely to be included in the final composition. For example, the Purple Sandpiper working its way down the slope headfirst had been a part of each and every arrangement I had considered. I carved it first.

The piece was off to a good start, but there were still occasional setbacks. I finished up a model of a sleeping turnstone one morning and set it in the small oven in my studio that I use to bake polymer clay. I made a quick trip to the house while the oven preheated. When I returned a few minutes later, I discovered smoke pouring out the door. The heating coil had broken, the oven had spiked to 1,000°, and my lovely little turnstone was burnt to a crisp. While it no longer says "turnstone," I find the shape quite interesting in terms of pure form.

Top: Ruddy Turnstones and Purple Sandpipers clay studies
polymer clay
Bottom: *Sleeping Turnstone*
overfired polymer clay
2000

PHOTO BY ALAN WYCHECK

PHOTO BY ALAN WYCHECK

shed in 1788 by a letter from John Wesley, Bristol, England

ITAGE UNITED METHODIST CHURCH

LIGONIER, PENNSYLVANIA

Phone 724-238-2627

keep base small
increases "crowd"

As late as February 27 (confirmed by the drawing on a dated church bulletin), with only two months remaining before the Ward Show deadline in April, I was still including three turnstones in the composition. The image looked good on paper, but I couldn't balance it in three dimensions. I was still trying to make the piece big. My new "more with less" approach required rethinking the old proportions. In the original composition of a dozen birds, the turnstones had outnumbered the sandpipers nine to three. When I reduced the piece, I had maintained that same ratio: nine to three became three to one. Compositionally, the single Purple Sandpiper was having a hard time holding his own against three bigger, showier birds.

In order to balance the smaller composition, I switched from multiple turnstones to a single turnstone, and at the same time switched from a single sandpiper to a pair. I pulled two turnstones I had already carved out of the composition and added another sandpiper.

With the composition finally resolved, it was full speed ahead!

Top: Turnstones and sandpipers conceptual sketch
ballpoint pen on church bulletin
February 27, 2000
Bottom: Working model for *Tidal Companions*
polymer clay
2000

It's April. The timeline is speeding up again, now counting by the day. With less than a month to go, every day makes a difference.

My goal is to finish the piece in time to take it to the Ward Show, the last weekend in April. The competitive aspect of the Ward Show is far less important to me than it once was. The show for me is a motivational device. It's a helpful deadline that I can use to force myself to get a piece done.

As the deadline nears, the pace quickens. No more leisurely walks between the house and studio. I trot back and forth and take the studio stairs two or three at a time. At first there are fewer breaks, then shorter breaks, and finally, no breaks at all. If I didn't like what I was doing, the situation would be intolerable. Fortunately, I love what I do. The long hours don't bother me. I am reminded of Andrew Carnegie's great line, "My heart is in the work."

When I really get going, totally immersed and working nonstop for eighteen or more hours a day, I develop a fluency with the work that I simply can't achieve working "regular" hours. I become very efficient. No time is wasted getting warmed up because I'm running hot all the time. It's not necessary to get back into it since I never back away.

Test sheets
gesso and acrylic on card stock
each 8½ x 11

100

Once the birds are carved, textured, and primed, they are ready for paint. At the same time I prime the birds, I also prime a few pieces of card stock, which become my test sheets. I test my color mixes and plan my painting strategy on these sheets rather than directly on my carving.

The sheets allow me to experiment freely and to try different approaches without risk until I find what will work best. I use them throughout the entire painting process and keep them, with the sheets from all the other birds that I've done, as a record of what has worked and what has not.

Painting is the final task. When the painting is done, the piece is finished. I laid my brush down at 8:30 P.M. on April 27, the night before the Ward World Championship. The shorebirds were finally done. I packed up quickly and drove all night to get back to Ocean City where I had seen the birds for the first time *exactly* twenty-five years and one day earlier. I arrived in time to enter my piece in the competition early the next morning. *Tidal Companions* won the "Best in World" title the following day.

So how long did it take? Four months? Or twenty-five years? I think the answer is <u>both</u>.

Tidal Companions is 12 inches high, 12 inches wide, and 10 inches deep, but what it represents is much bigger than that. It *represents* a mixed flock of shorebirds and the rocky setting that surrounds them. Although the actual piece of sculpture can fit inside a small box, the scene it represents can fill an entire field of view.

The concept of a piece of sculpture *representing* the subject rather than actually *being* the subject eluded me at first. Only after I realized this concept was I able to open myself to the idea of a smaller version of my original idea.

The key to resolving *Tidal Companions'* composition—the key to distilling what was originally such a large and complex image down to its simplest terms—lay in the realization that one turnstone was enough.

A flock of turnstones is an arresting sight. I had always thought I would need to include as many birds as I could in order to convey the same visual drama provided by an entire flock. But an individual Ruddy Turnstone is so boldly colored and patterned that even a single bird declares "turnstone" in no uncertain terms. One bird, all by itself, is enough to firmly establish the idea of turnstone.

In a composition that was reduced to the bare essentials, one turnstone was all I needed.

Somewhere, buried deep in a closet, I still had the rocks and barnacles I had gathered in Maine years before. I dug them out and rediscovered what had drawn me to them twenty years earlier. I had indeed found the perfect rock. And now that the piece had become so much smaller than what I had originally planned, I had a rock I could use as a model that was just the right size, too. Usually when you finally find an item that's been in the closet for twenty years, it isn't as nice as you remembered —this time it was.

The rock's dark green color worked well with the turnstone and with the Purple Sandpipers individually, and then tied all the birds—and the whole piece—together as well. It provides a dark backdrop, enabling the light barnacles to stand out as highlights that punctuate the composition with a bit of lyrical rhythm.

The composition of *Tidal Companions* is a subset of the very same elements I had been excited about for many years. The new challenge had become to rearrange those elements so that each one, in the final composition, could do double duty representing not just itself, but the rest of the imagined scene as well.

I still daydream about doing the big version of this piece, one with a dozen birds, waves, and rockweed . . . Perhaps someday I will do the piece as large as I envisioned it originally. If I ever do, then *Tidal Companions* will become part of an even longer timeline.

BROAD-WINGED HAWK

Buteo platypterus

A close encounter

An idea starts with a source of inspiration. Building on some spark, it grows and develops and takes on a life of its own. Every idea has a lifespan—a period of time during which I am enthusiastic about the idea and its potential. Some ideas have long lives and some have shorter ones. An idea's lifespan is determined by a host of variables that are specific to that particular idea, to my thinking at the time, and to the direction of my work.

I find that if I don't act on an idea within its lifespan, the urgency fades, the idea can weaken and die, and whatever chance that particular idea might have had is lost. This is not necessarily a bad thing. I do not mourn the passing of ideas that never came into being for two reasons. The first is that new ideas are arriving constantly to take their place. The second is that not every idea is a good one. Often the ideas that have shorter lifespans turn out to be less worthy ones. If I were working in a more spontaneous medium, I would be far more willing to take on ideas as they come, to try them in order to see if they might work. But the time-consuming nature of my work and my limited output require that I consider very carefully before I commit to my next project.

My slow and deliberate methods cause most of my ideas to spend a long time simmering, waiting patiently for their day to come. The benefit of this way of working is that as time passes, the ideas with shorter lifespans fall by the wayside. What are left are the ideas that won't go away, do not fade, and will not die. The ideas that interest me are the ones that grow over time rather than diminish. The majority of my pieces are derived from ideas that have been waiting in the wings for a long time—ideas that have been revised, revisited, reviewed, and refined and still hold my interest even after the passage of many years. Ideas that I come back to, again and again.

The inspiration for my sculpture of a Broad-winged Hawk came when I almost hit a very real hawk while driving home from the opening of the annual "Birds in Art" exhibition at the Leigh Yawkey Woodson Art Museum in Wausau, Wisconsin. I always leave "Birds in Art" in a state of heightened awareness brought on by the stimulation provided by the work, the artists, and the museum itself. When an adult Broad-winged Hawk flew low across the road just inches from my bumper, I was in the perfect position, mentally and physically, to take in the sight. (The flat face of a Volkswagen bus affords a particularly good view of anything that you almost hit.) The hawk was spectacular. That close encounter sparked an idea that grew and matured slowly over the next twenty years . . . an idea that became better and better with the passage of time.

106

Broad-winged Hawk
38 x 22 x 24
acrylic on basswood
2001

I was completely taken with the image of a Broad-winged Hawk in flight and immediately began thinking about how to translate what I had seen into a carving. In my early conceptual sketches, I replaced the car's bumper and the road's asphalt with a weathered snag and a bit of leafy greenery. I placed a snake in the bird's talons, thinking that it could trail downward to somehow provide the means of contact necessary to support the bird in flight. My sketches were rough, but they gave the idea form and substance. Once the idea was established on paper, I could set it aside without fear of losing it.

My initial encounter with the bird had occurred in 1981. I did not do the piece until 2001. During the intervening twenty years, the intent and emphasis of my work changed. Design and presentation had become increasingly more important to me. And while the craftsmanship, technical skill, and detail involved still mattered, I no longer thought of flawless execution as the goal. Instead, I saw technique as the means to reach for new goals. I still carved birds, but I wanted the birds to be a part of an artistic whole that would be seen, first and foremost, as a piece of sculpture.

I start out using a bird's features and feathers to establish the unique contours that are responsible for conveying the ring of truth about the particular bird I am working on. In this case, that means identifying the subtle but specific shapes, forms, and proportions that make a Broad-winged Hawk immediately identifiable as a Broad-winged Hawk and set it apart from all the other hawks that may be similar but each of which has its own set of individual characteristics. It is critical that I be able to identify the intrinsic and distinctive attributes that are tied to my subject's identity so that I can then work to establish those same distinctive qualities in my carving.

Once the overall contours have been determined and the attitude of the bird has been established, I begin to play with the layout of the feathers themselves. There is quite a bit of structure associated with feathers. Each individual feather consists of barbs neatly arranged on either side of a central shaft. A feather's shape relates to its function and location on the bird. Feathers do not grow randomly, but in well-defined tracts that bring a sense of order to a bird's appearance. Feathers are orderly, but not overly so. There is a lot of room for playful arrangement, and I delight in the rhythm and flow of plumage. I use the feathers to enhance and accentuate the underlying shapes and forms. What begins as a representation of a specific bird gradually, and inevitably, becomes a celebration of the shape, pattern, and geometry of feathers.

Traditionally, color and light are considered to be the concerns of the painter, while the sculptor deals with the issues of shape and form. In reality, the distinction between the two disciplines is not always so clean cut. In my work, I find there is no separation between the two concerns whatsoever; I deal with both. In fact, it is exactly where the concerns of the two-dimensional painter and the three-dimensional sculptor meet and overlap that I spend the majority of my time. I use the tools of both camps, and I wouldn't have it any other way. The manner in which the colors and patterns found in the plumage of birds relate to the shapes and forms of birds intrigues and fascinates me as much as any other aspect of what I do. The bolder the patterns, the more I enjoy finding ways to reconcile those patterns with the shapes and forms that lie beneath them. A feather's markings provide the means to define the edge of an individual feather or an entire group. Pattern accentuates the way feathers lie or roll to meet their neighbors. Bars and streaks can call attention to a gentle contour, enhance a shape, or reveal a subtle curve. The paint accentuates the form and, in turn, the form accentuates the paint. The interplay between the two, combined with texture, sets up a dynamic that allows the surface to truly come alive.

It may sound backward, but the tighter the feather detail gets, the more abstract my thinking becomes. And it must if the subject is to remain fresh and lifelike. Including as much detail as I do, I run the risk of turning the entire project stiff and dry. The longer I work on a piece, the greater the risk. If I labor for six months or more, how do I keep it looking fresh, when to me it no longer is? I am convinced that the loose, abstract way I handle feathers is the key. Feathers grow in orderly rows, but I rarely present them in such a regimented fashion. In my mind, the feathers become abstract elements of design that I use to create interest and movement. As I vary spacing and intervals, lines form and rhythms develop. Things are always on the move, either coming together or drifting apart. Shapes merge into patterns, break up, and then reform. There is a casual sense of composition in my feathers rather than a perfectly ordered symmetry. I want the bird to appear comfortable but not disheveled, as if he has simply "loosened his tie." I'd like the bird to project a natural beauty rather than appear to be an object that has been made by man.

I can get lost in an area like the one pictured here. When I get the chance to study an area like this on a real bird, or to work my way through it on a bird that I am carving, I feel myself getting drawn in, and, for a time, a few square inches of feathers become my whole world. I start out identifying the different feather groups, such as the axillaries or the rows of coverts that make up the wing lining. I move on to note the various characteristics of the individual feathers. I follow the transitions from shape to shape, from one color to another, from one pattern to the next, as a bar becomes a chevron, which in turn becomes a streak. At a certain point it becomes less about the detail of feathers and simply an abstract expression of rhythm and flow.

When I look at an area like this, I see music. I hear and feel the steady rhythm of a bass line overlaid with the rise and fall of brighter notes and melody. I feel cadence and beat; I see harmonies and duets, flourishes and crescendos; and I sense sparkling grace notes rising up and hovering over a small avian symphony.

Detail is just that: detail. The integrity of the concept as a whole is more important than the detail that supports it. When detail and design are properly balanced and working in harmony, then detail falls into its proper role—subservient to the whole while adding richness, texture, and interest to a composition that would still be strong without it.

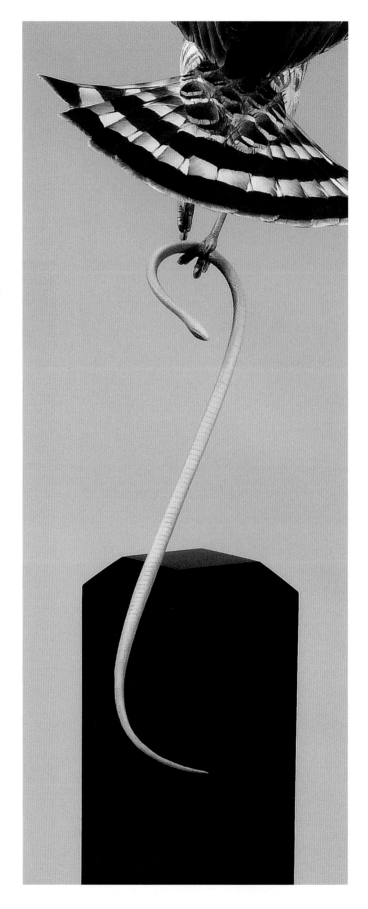

My original sketch from twenty years earlier looked like a bird carving. I wanted it to look more like a piece of sculpture. I eliminated the driftwood and leaves. With the snag and leaves gone, the piece was no longer tied to the earth by plants and stumps rooted in the ground. Although I had originally seen the bird a foot off the ground, I wanted the viewer to envision the bird flying free. I replaced the low, turned base in the old sketch with a tall black plinth that gave the composition a stronger sculptural presence and enabled the viewer to envision the bird at any height. In the original sketch, a black-and-white ribbon snake trailed down and made contact with the leaves below. In the revised composition, I eliminated all vegetation. Switching to the green snake enabled me to suggest the hawk's leafy woodland setting without actually including any leaves. The snake's color complements the hawk's coloration the same way that leaves would have.

The line of the snake was inspired by the gesture of a particularly elegant curly fry. I was able to rescue the fry just as my children were about to pull it apart. It had a natural grace that would have been difficult to make up without seeming contrived. It was pinned to my studio wall for years until the mice finished it off. Inspiration really can come from anywhere at any time.

A close encounter had inspired me to carve a Broad-winged Hawk, but simply duplicating what I had seen was not the answer. A flying hawk attached to a bumper would have been accurate but would have made a poor piece of sculpture. For me, a good design always includes a thoughtful, deliberate, and intentional reordering of the elements in the composition rather than simply repeating what I've seen.

WINTER SANDERLINGS

Calidris alba

Defying gravity

Subject matter is a personal choice that reflects the interests of each individual artist. The medium an artist selects—watercolor, oils, or acrylics; bronze, clay, wood, or stone; ink, graphite, or anything else—is also a personal choice. Certain subjects lend themselves more easily to certain mediums. In turn, the idiosyncratic traits of a medium—both its strengths and its limitations—affect how an artist will approach and present a subject. Bronze, for example, might be an ideal medium for an artist drawn to the powerful shapes of elephants, moose, and buffalo, but likely not the first (or best) choice for an artist captivated by cloudscapes, morning light, and rising mist. There are exceptions, of course. Art does not survive by being predictable. An artist who can make sense out of something that makes no sense to anyone else might just be onto something big. Exciting things can happen when a creative person disregards what he or she is supposed to do and then succeeds in doing precisely what was thought could not be done.

Wood is a good medium for sculpting birds. It is soft enough to carve easily, yet hard enough to hold detail well. Its structure and grain lend themselves to the carving and texturing of feathers. Feathers and wood share a comparable ratio of lightness and strength. There is an inherent softness and warmth in wood that enables it to effectively communicate the softness and warmth I see in birds' plumage. At the same time, wood can convey the exacting precision and functionality found in an open wing or a hard, sharp beak. Both wood and birds have a roughly similar weight and density. A carved bird has a heft that seems right. It feels good in my hand.

Although wood serves me well in my ongoing effort to capture and present the beauty I see in birds, there are times when I look at other mediums with some longing and envy. I must admit, I am a bit jealous of the ease with which a painter can do certain things that a sculptor cannot. If a painter wants to suspend a bird in flight, he or she can simply place the bird in the sky and it is done. A bird running with both feet off the ground needs only a shadow beneath it and poof, it is airborne. In a painting, no thought is required as to how a bird is held aloft, while in sculpture the contacts and connections necessary to support anything that isn't firmly on the ground are a constant concern.

Winter Sanderlings
5 x 14 x 10
acrylic on tupelo
2002

Winter Sanderlings was the result of wanting to do what can't be done. I wanted to find a sculptural solution that would allow me to present a bird up and off the ground with no visible means of support.

Only three of the many legs in the flock make contact with the ground. They touch down and form a tripod that supports the piece. A series of brass tabs and receiving slots runs through the flock, connecting the individual birds. Two of the birds have no contact with the ground whatsoever, only with the birds around them. One is in the middle of the tripod; it binds together the three birds that form the tripod and, in turn, is supported by them. The other is suspended outside of the tripod and cantilevers out to the right side of the group while the weight of the four other birds keeps the piece from tipping over.

Sanderlings seem to lift the spirits of everyone who comes across them. At the right time of year, they are found running nimbly up and down sandy beaches, moving in and out at the very edge of the surf. They relentlessly follow the advance and retreat of the sea, hoping to find a bit of food exposed for an instant by each receding wave. Their boundless energy, as they run and run as fast as their tiny legs can carry them, is comical and endearing. It's impossible to walk a beach with a small group of Sanderlings running on ahead without feeling that the time shared with these delightful birds has been special.

This was a fun piece to do. The cheerful energy of the birds themselves and the lively exuberance of the presentation made every aspect of the entire project a delight.

The concept of *Winter Sanderlings*—and the whole reason to do this piece—is represented in the single bird you see here. This bird is running fast, with both feet off the ground. It levitates with no visible means of support. The bird's only contact with the ground below is its own shadow. All the joinery necessary to connect the birds and support the piece is out of sight, invisibly absorbed by the slight body-to-body contact between the birds as they run together in a tight, compact group.

A theater stage crew that does its job well is invisible. Flawless execution draws no attention to itself, and the audience focuses on the performance rather than on the production details. The success of *Winter Sanderlings* depends on a similar illusion of effortlessness. A lot is going on behind the scenes, but I hope I have handled the technique discreetly enough that the pure delight and whimsical nature of these wonderful birds take center stage.

My Sanderling flock includes five birds. Drilling leg holes in the right spots and at the correct angles can be difficult even for a single bird. I rarely get it right on the first try. Most of my birds have far more holes drilled in them than the two that are required. I thought working out the location and position of ten legs was going to be a nightmare, but it went more easily than I had anticipated, thanks to a simple trick I learned back in grade school.

As kids, we amused ourselves by drawing short, animated sequences in the bottom corners of our school tablets and then rapidly flipping through the pages to watch the action. I determined the leg positions of the Sanderlings in the very same way. The leg positions of the five birds are what you would draw in a simple flip chart to represent a running bird. Starting at the back of the pack and moving forward, the birds are running along sequentially, just as they would in our tablets. This simple device animates the piece and brings a sense of order and rhythm to the many lines and angles in the churning legs of the little flock. I had used a similar approach to animate *Bering Sea Pirates* with a wingbeat moving through the piece. My running Sanderlings is the ground version.

It seems everyone familiar with Sanderlings is
fond of them. They make us smile. "Whimsical"
is not a word I would normally use to describe my
work, but in the case of *Winter Sanderlings*, it fits.

RED-BILLED TROPICBIRD

Phaethon aethereus

"Never let the facts get in the way of a good story." —Mark Twain

My primary artistic concern can, and often does, change from piece to piece. As I work on a piece, I may find myself engaged with a particular sculptural issue, such as color, texture, or movement. That issue may rise up and take on a major role. With the next piece, I might move in an entirely different direction, and that same issue may no longer be as relevant or seem as important as it once did. I may disregard it entirely.

I talk consistently about the importance of detail and accuracy in my work. I go on and on about the beauty and perfection of birds and my desire to present them as faithfully as I can. I speak of my work's being a response to things I have seen, of its being the result of connections and experiences I've had with a particular bird or species I have known well for many years. I refer over and over to the importance of field work and knowing the subject.

And then I carve a Red-billed Tropicbird—a bird I have never seen.

As far as I know, I've never even been close to one. I have had no field experience with them and I have no firsthand knowledge of them whatsoever. In fact, I know very little about them other than what I have read

in books. But I do know this: they are simply spectacular. And there are days when that alone is enough.

I think it's safe to say I have considered the sculptural possibilities of every bird I've met. It is simply an automatic response on my part, to imagine how every bird I see lends itself to sculpture. I am constantly picturing the ways a bird could be presented, considering possibilities, weighing options, and searching for solutions. This includes not just the birds I see in the field, but also any I come across in books and photographs.

Although I had never seen a live one, Red-billed Tropicbirds had been on my mind for a long time. I made a small clay study of a tropicbird years ago, but never took it any further because I was not comfortable sculpting a bird I had never seen. The little clay study moved from place to place in my studio for fifteen years. Eventually, the sculptural potential of the bird's dramatic form and bold pattern proved to be irresistible. I decided not to let my lack of familiarity with the subject keep me from doing a piece I felt so strongly about. *Red-billed Tropicbird* represents an artistic story that was just too good not to be told.

Red-billed Tropicbird
44 x 12 x 13
acrylic on basswood
2003

There are over 6,000 different species of birds on our planet. I will see only a small fraction of them in my lifetime, and there are even fewer that I'll have the chance to carve. But there are very few that I have not at least *thought* about carving.

Every time I'd thought about tropicbirds over the years, I had imagined a dramatic vertical composition. The idea of going vertical wasn't based on any first-hand knowledge of tropicbirds; in fact, it contradicted what little I did know about them. In all the photographs I had seen, the tropicbird's long tail feathers were always streaming out behind the bird horizontally. But in spite of that—and perhaps precisely because I didn't know the bird well enough to know any better—I continued to cling to the idea of the bird's long tail feathers going up instead of out. One thing I did know was that tropicbirds nest on sea cliffs. It seemed likely that a bird perched on a small bit of ledge and backed up against a rock face might hold its tail straight up in the vertical composition I had in mind.

Normally when I work out the design of a piece, I rely on my field sketches and experience with the live bird, and perhaps a number of samples I may have collected. In this case, I had very little in the way of support material. I was taking all my cues directly from the bird's flamboyant shape and the abstract quality of its graphic black-and-white plumage.

What is important to me changes from piece to piece. With *Red-billed Tropicbird*, what had become important was the visual impact of the bird itself. It had nothing to do with any personal experience I'd had with a tropicbird. It was simply a bird that looked so good to me that I wanted to spend more time with it. I wanted to see what I could do with it and where I could take it sculpturally.

While I worked on this composition, natural history took a backseat to the pure aesthetics of form and design. Initially, I had been hesitant to step away from the standard of accuracy that has always been such an important part of my work. But I found it very liberating to design and sculpt unencumbered by the constraints of what the bird does or doesn't do. I was able to revel in the glory of the bird itself, without having to stick to a viable storyline dictated by natural history. This allowed me to let the powerful abstract qualities of the bird's pattern, color, and form determine the direction of the piece and the composition.

For many years the open bill of the tropic-bird presented an obstacle that kept me from moving ahead with the piece. I didn't know what the inside looked like. It would have been much easier if I had kept the bill closed, but that was not an option I was willing to consider. The bill simply had to be open.

To justify the vertical tail feathers, I had backed the bird up against a wall and into a corner. Its posture carries the hint of an implied threat. The open bill reinforces the bird's defensive stance, but more importantly, it serves to balance the composition in the round. In terms of abstract design, the piece consists of a central mass with linear elements working out away from the center in pairs. The two tail feathers stretch upward into the space above the piece, the two crossed wingtips into the space behind. The two wrists aim ahead, low and wide. The bill needed to be open to form two elements—the upper and lower portions—to advance up and out into the space in front of the piece.

It's very likely there are some out there who will see the tropicbird I've carved and think that I got the bill all wrong. If they know tropicbirds, then they might be right. I would have liked to have talked to them while I was working on the piece. I freely admit I took some creative liberties. While it may not be accurate in the strictest sense, my solution was based on more than a hunch: it was based on my knowledge of birds in general and the familiarity I have with related species that have similar habits.

In the end, I came to realize that the detail in the open bill was less important than the overall design and impact of the piece as a whole.

I cheat more and more all the time. Perhaps "cheat" is too strong a word—let's say I am increasingly willing to stretch the truth. Early on, when I was first learning about birds and how to carve them, I was far more exacting. I'm still learning, and always will be, but at this point I know enough to start bending the rules. I may make a bird bigger than it really is or a wing longer than it is, or alter a bird in any number of other ways in order to enhance its appearance and strengthen the composition it is a part of. Now, the impression of accuracy is enough. It is more important to me that the bird look right than be right.

There are times when I knowingly deviate from a literal depiction of a bird in order to be more faithful to my artistic vision. At such times, I follow Twain's advice to never let the facts get in the way of a good story.

WIND RIVER HARMONY

Mountain Bluebirds & Juniper

A balancing act

Which came first, the chicken or the egg? There really isn't an answer. But in the end, it doesn't really matter, because the question's real value lies in the thought process it triggers.

When it comes to sculpture, I find it useful to ask a slightly different question: Which came first, the bird or the idea? The value of the question remains the same—it makes me think a little harder about what I'm doing and why I'm doing it. It makes me more deliberate in my decision-making and helps me stay focused on what is important.

Sometimes it is the bird that provides me with the starting point of a piece, and I build a design around a particular species. Sometimes an idea comes first, and I later incorporate the bird whose attributes best support the concept. Every once in a great while, the bird and the idea arrive simultaneously in a blinding flash, but this is rare in my experience. Even when a perfect combination seems to fall into my lap, I still must wrestle with many compositional decisions in order to transform that bit of inspiration into an effective piece of sculpture.

When I begin to work on a project of my own choosing, I usually start with an idea and then select the bird best suited to it. The process tends to move in the opposite direction when I work on a commission.

Usually a client has a specific bird in mind. My job is to come up with a design that best uses that bird's qualities. Neither method is better than the other; they simply approach the same objective from opposite directions. The goal is to unite a strong bird with a strong idea to create a strong piece. It is usually easier for me to figure out what bird goes best with an established idea than it is to come up with a great idea for a pre-established bird. The number of birds is finite and I can find my choices close at hand in the nearest field guide, but there is no field guide to good ideas. Coming up with a good idea for a piece is often the most challenging aspect of the entire process.

Through the years, I've worked on a number of pieces and approached them from both directions. I have learned it is difficult to proceed with enthusiasm unless I am just as excited about the design of the piece as I am about the particular species involved. For me, design and composition are critical components of a piece and must receive as much, or more, consideration as the choice of subject matter. Ultimately, I have come to the conclusion that the element of design is the most important part of the entire process. In art, the choice of subject matter does not determine worth or success; it is what an artist does with subject matter that counts.

Wind River Harmony
32 x 12 x 12
acrylic on basswood
2008

At the center of the piece, the quiet females are nestled in the center of the juniper. Your eye rests on them because they rest. The juniper rises around them and leads your eye up to the male bird above. The sky-blue male is high in the composition, exactly where the sky should be. His outstretched wings are like an umbrella that caps the piece, gathering in the juniper's upward motion. Your eye then drifts back down to gently settle once again upon the females resting below.

I see the piece as two overlapping triangular shapes, one pointing up and the other down. One represents the juniper and the other the birds. Within the juniper shape, color moves from a wide, deep, green base up to the neutral gray spires of the dead branches at the top. The birds offer the reverse. The intense color of the male with his wings spread wide up high gives way to the neutral earth tones of the females below. Considered separately, each transition is heavily weighted at one end or the other, but together they balance the piece from top to bottom. The neutral branches don't compete with the male's bright color, and the females' subdued tones receive the color support they need to match the male's intensity.

139

Bluebirds have a tendency to gather in small, loose flocks during the months outside of the nesting season. *Wind River Harmony* was meant to convey the easy, comfortable dynamics of just such a group. One bird would not have been enough to carry the idea of a flock. It was my intention to include both male and female plumage in the piece, but just two birds, one male and one female, would have been seen as a mated pair and shifted the feel of the piece to the nesting season. Three birds was the minimum number required to represent the informal group I had in mind. Two males and one female was an option, but a single female's somber plumage would have been difficult to balance against two brightly colored males. One male and two females gave me the best chance to work out a harmonious composition.

I wanted the individual birds to have a casual awareness of each other but nothing more. The birds are quite close to one another, but having them avoid any direct eye contact lessened the chance that the viewer would assume a relationship I did not intend.

Male and female Mountain Bluebirds are both stunning, but each gender makes its impact in a very different way. The female's soft, subtle beauty lends itself to a quiet and restful piece, while the bold electric-blue of the male calls for action and movement.

These personalities were so different that I considered two separate companion pieces at one point, one quiet and the other active, but in the end I brought both approaches together and enjoyed the way they complemented each other. I chose to portray two females and one male in order to balance the attention each would receive. Together, the two females create a visual impact equal to that of the more vibrant and active male. What the females lack in color and animation, they make up for in numbers.

Art is a constant search for equilibrium, an ongoing effort to bring dissimilar elements into balance. It is a search that never ends. Nor should it, for it is the tension between opposing forces—and the constant struggle to balance those forces—that makes art dynamic and powerful.

141

I had made the artistic decision to place the bluebirds in juniper without regard to the very significant technical concerns of how to actually make juniper. It's quite common for me to decide *what* to do first, trusting that I will be able to figure out the *how* later.

Juniper was a bigger challenge than most. After a lot of trial and error, I built what, as far as I know, is the world's only juniper jig. It's a 10-foot-long monstrosity that requires three people to operate. I cut an old bicycle apart and mounted a free-spinning wheel rim at each end of a 10-foot plank. Centered between the wheels is a device that looks like a cross between a set of medieval thumbscrews and a miniature cider press. The device holds two knurling heads against each other. Knurling heads are used in metal lathes to press a diamond pattern onto the handles and shafts. I drew bronze rod down to the wire size I needed and attached it to the wheel rims with cables. My helpers, one turning each wheel, ran the wire back and forth while I held the wire in tension as it passed between the knurling heads. The heads pressed a diagonal pattern into the wire. I needed a lot of wire. Any family, friends, or visitors who came even close to my studio were pressed into service, but the task fell primarily to my wife and daughter.

The sole purpose of the jig was simply to give my wire stock some texture. I still needed to weld the wire together and form it into juniper. When the finished juniper was painted, the diagonal pattern caught the light and made a subtle but critical difference. It would not have looked like juniper without it.

Speaking as a bird carver, I'd say *Wind River Harmony* is about Mountain Bluebirds and juniper. But as an artist and sculptor, I am more inclined to say that the piece is about bringing opposites together to form a balanced whole.

KILLDEER

Charadrius vociferus

Providing an opening

Normally I shy away from portraying a bird in any type of ritualistic display. Courtship in the world of birds is filled with curious behaviors and outlandish displays. Such rituals often involve exaggerated poses that, while fascinating to see in person, do not appeal to me as subjects for sculpture. As a student of natural history, I find many of these behaviors interesting and quite remarkable, but as a sculptor, I find them to be ungainly and awkwardly unnatural. The bizarre postures may be effective in drawing the attention of prospective mates, but to me, the displays seem artificial, stilted, comical, or just plain silly. Too often, they seem to contradict, rather than enhance, the natural beauty and form of the bird. And the amount of time a bird spends in a display posture is so small compared to how it appears day in and day out that it seems wrong to concentrate on an unnatural posture in which the bird spends so little time.

I feel quite differently, though, about the distraction display of the Killdeer. The Killdeer routinely feigns injury to distract a predator or any other threat away from its nest. The bird flutters along ahead of the intruder, dragging one wing (or both) and its tail, listing to one side and quivering pitifully, crying all the while in an effort to be as visually tantalizing as possible. The Killdeer's broken-wing act is a deliberate attempt to draw attention. The bird makes itself the center of interest and then uses that attention to lead the threat away from the nest. Rather than an odd, rarely seen courtship display, a Killdeer's broken-wing act is often what brings the bird to our attention and, for many, is the time when the bird is most likely to be seen. The bird's display is not intended to attract the attention of a potential mate—it is intended to attract us!

Again, as a student of natural history, I find it interesting to speculate on whether the bird does this on purpose, with conscious intent, or if its behavior is the result of being caught between the need to stay and protect its young and the need to flee and protect itself. But it makes little difference to me as an artist. What attracts me, first and foremost, is the visual feast of the bird itself as it exposes its beauty in such a flamboyant manner. What a perfect subject for sculpture. In order for the ruse to be successful, the bird must be bold, dramatic, and eye-catching. The bird's display lends itself to—and reinforces so well—the same goals I have as an artist. Like the Killdeer, it is my intention to create a powerful image that will catch the viewer's eye and rivet his or her attention.

Killdeer
Bird: 7 x 11 x 11
Nest: $1^1/_2$ x $4^1/_2$ x $4^1/_2$
acrylic on basswood and maple
2009

The piece I'd had in mind originally was far more elaborate. An early conceptual sketch shows I had envisioned a long sweep of rocky ground and stubble bridging the distance between the bird and the nest. In the end, I chose to eliminate the connection and present both the bird and the nest separately, with empty space between them. The empty space is an invitation to viewers to fill in the gap between the bird and nest with information that comes from their own life experiences: places they know, places they have been, and encounters they might have had with Killdeer.

The presentation of my Killdeer and nest affected how people reacted to the piece and how they talked to me about it. Every time I've shown this piece, people have shared more stories than usual with me. This piece prompts people to tell me about their own encounters with Killdeer. They've told me about the Killdeer displaying at the golf course, the bird next to the soccer field, the one carrying on in a hotel parking lot, in the middle of a driveway, next to the ferry landing, at a rest stop, in a pasture, along the river—each of the situations related to me have been different, but they have all ended the same way. The storytellers looked back at my piece and said, " . . . and it looked just like that!"

What I had carved, my bird and my nest, had been enough to start the process, but it was the empty space between them that allowed the viewers to relate to it in a very personal way and make the piece their own.

Not everyone's experience with a feigning Killdeer includes the nest. The bird's display indicates the eggs or chicks are near, but the whole point of the bird's actions is to keep you from discovering the exact location. Whenever I see a bird performing a broken-wing act, I immediately begin treading very, very lightly and scanning the ground in all directions. Searching for the nest is part of the charm of such an encounter. It is a delight to actually find it, but as often as not the eggs or chicks go undetected.

Presenting the nest separately seemed to more accurately convey the dynamics of the situation. Floating the nest without a fixed and predetermined relationship with the bird maintained a certain degree of ambiguity that enhanced the viewers' ability to read into the situation what they wanted to, to see what they wanted to see. My bird and nest may sit three or four feet apart, but without a direct and literal connection, the viewer is free to imagine them being separated by any distance and terrain.

I put a lot of detail in my sculpture in an effort to do justice to the rich plumage of birds, their clean, precise faces, their lovely eyes, and their exquisitely shaped bills and feet. The detail I include contains so much visual information that the sheer volume can, at times, overwhelm the communication that takes place between the viewer and the piece. The high degree of realism can leave very little room for interpretation. If everything has been so completely and thoroughly resolved, there is little left for the viewer to do but take it in.

As a result, the exchange between the piece and the viewer can become one-sided. It's all too easy for the information to move from the piece to the viewer in only one direction, like traffic on a one-way street. But it isn't really a conversation if one side is doing all the talking. I want to encourage a more lively exchange. I look for ways to provide an opening, to include some form of empty space, some element or ingredient intentionally left unresolved that can serve as an invitation to the viewer to fill in the blank space with information from his or her life experiences. I'd like the relationship between the viewer and my work to become more like a two-way street. When the viewer is able to bring something to the conversation and add to the information I have provided, the bond between the piece and the viewer becomes much stronger and more meaningful.

The bright color of the Killdeer's rump and the pattern in its wings and tail are normally hidden from sight. The bird shows them to bring attention to itself. I have used those very attributes to draw attention to my sculpture, which returns the focus to the starting point: the bird itself.

MARSH HAWK

Northern Harrier & Reeds

The power of flight

I can only go so long before I am lured back, once again, to the idea of putting a bird in the air. This is no surprise. Of all the characteristics and qualities we associate with birds, the one that stands out above the rest is their ability to fly. It is in the flawless, exquisite grace of avian flight that we see the ultimate expression of the elegant beauty and perfection of birds. So I return to the theme of flight again and again.

The mechanics of flight are complex. Understanding them is made all the more difficult because the live models simply will not stay still. Birds in flight are always on the move. There are exceptions: hummingbirds and some others can hover in place, but in order to do so they beat their wings so fast that you still can't see what's going on. The downstroke is the simpler part of a wingbeat. In larger birds, it is slow enough that it can be perceived with the naked eye. The upstroke is much faster and more complex. So much happens so quickly during the recovery stroke that high-speed photography is required to see and fully understand what is taking place. I lean toward the clean simplicity of the downstroke.

In my own work, I favor the attitudes of flight that involve set wings rather than a lot of wild, energetic flapping. The more animated a pose, the greater the discrepancy between the real bird, which actually does move, and my sculpture, which does not. I find this discrepancy unsettling and look for ways to soften the contrast. One option is to select simpler poses in the first place. Poses that involve a more limited range of motion are easier to achieve believably and hold up in the long run. For example, I find the long, slow glide of a flock of geese coming in to be more poetic and somehow more accessible visually than the chaotic frenzy of that same flock taking off. The frenzied takeoff is very exciting in the moment, but the calmer tranquility of the gentle landing stays with me longer.

A piece of sculpture does not tire, but the people who look at it do. When I place a bird in flight, I like the bird to look as though it could hold its position for a long time without strain. If the bird looks uncomfortable, I think it can make the viewer uneasy as well. The more energetic the pose, the sooner the viewer may feel the need to take a break, to move on and rest. The more serene a piece, the more likely the viewer will slow down, enjoy the peace and quiet and calm tranquility, and linger.

Marsh Hawk
49 x 27 x 25
acrylic on basswood and tupelo
2010

Marsh Hawk is a life-size version of a piece that was originally envisioned on a much smaller scale. Every spring, Bobolinks return to the local hayfields. They are gifted singers, with a unique song that has been described as reckless, rollicking, effervescent, and irrepressible. Best of all, they deliver it on the wing. The males pour out their exuberant song while flying low over the meadow grasses. As I have watched the birds floating over the fields, I've thought about ways to translate the image into sculpture. I had imagined a miniature meadow with a few grass heads reaching high enough to make contact with the singing bird flying just above it. I liked the concept and couldn't help but think about other birds that could take advantage of the same formula.

The time was right for a larger piece. I tried scaling up the idea of a Bobolink flying over a field of grass and translated it into a Marsh Hawk flying over a bed of reeds. Marsh Hawks are not the flashiest or best known of our raptors. They are not as fast as Peregrine Falcons or as powerful as Golden Eagles, but they are exceedingly graceful and elegant birds that have always appealed to me. I think their long wings are the most distinctively shaped and beautiful of all our birds of prey. Marsh Hawks are an ideal size, large enough to be impressive without being huge. Their size, appearance, habits, and behavior all fit together perfectly with the concept I had in mind, making them an ideal candidate for my next bird in flight.

Top: Bobolink
studio drawing
6 x 8
Bottom: Marsh Hawk
studio drawing
5 x 7

154

Officially, these birds are known as Northern Harriers, but Marsh Hawk is the name I grew up with and the one I still prefer. By either name, they are slim, graceful birds of prey with feeding habits that lend themselves nicely to a sculptural presentation. The birds fly low over a marsh just above the vegetation, ready to suddenly drop down upon anything that appears below. Their low flight provides options for dealing with the ever-present problem of how to support a bird in the air.

I started by making a wire mockup. My model was small and simple—a few pieces of wire tacked together, a small block of wood, and cut-out paper wings—but it was enough to give me a sense of how the concept was going to work in three dimensions. Even in the simple wire model, the lines that form the abstract core of the piece are already in place. The model is simple and unrefined, but it has the look and feel of the finished piece. Apart from paint and surface detail, the two are remarkably similar.

Compositionally, *Marsh Hawk* is built upon the balanced tension between two invisible lines of force. The more tangible of the two lines is defined by the forward direction of the flying bird. The second line is the direction of the wind. I can't carve wind, but I can bring it into the composition with the flow and bend of the reeds. The dynamic tension between the two opposing lines is what holds the entire composition together and gives it energy.

Top: Marsh Hawk wire model
paper, wood, and steel
11 x 8 x 6
Bottom: *Marsh Hawk* finished piece
49 x 27 x 25

I try to make the space around the piece as meaningful as the piece itself. This thinking applies to time as well as space. Along with the immediacy of the moment that I present, I want the viewer to have a sense of what came before and what will follow. I try to present a passage of time. A frozen instant loses something when it is removed from context. It loses momentum when separated from the sequence it was a part of. It is not my goal to capture and isolate a single split second. I don't want to stop the action. Quite to the contrary, I want to see to it that it continues. This is especially true with a bird in flight. A flying bird needs to be seen as part of a continuum. I want *Marsh Hawk* to convey a sense of buoyant flight, the bird quartering effortlessly over the marsh in a timeless way that could go on for hours.

Generally speaking, I strive to include any element that can broaden the focus rather than tighten and narrow it. There is already plenty of tightness in my work due to the high degree of realism and detail— what I need is more looseness. I look for ways to offset the strictly literal depiction with any form of openness that will allow the viewer to imagine a scene larger and longer than the one I have presented. Including a sense of continuance is another way of making the piece expand beyond its physical parameters.

158

I had a number of choices for plumage. Male and female Marsh Hawks are quite different in appearance. Young birds are similar to the female, but distinctive enough to offer a third option. I chose the silvery-gray coloration of an adult male. In my younger days, I would have been tempted by the plumage of the female and young birds, both of which are more heavily marked with streaks, bars, color, and pattern. Back then, I gravitated toward more complex feather patterns. Somewhere along the way, I found myself favoring simpler plumages. As I have grown as a sculptor, basic form has become more and more important to me. The shape of things has become of greater concern than the intricacies of surface detail. Many of the more cryptic patterns and colorations are designed by nature to conceal the bird's form, to hide it from detection. As a sculptor, my intent is to bring the form to the fore and reveal it. I am still fascinated with the texture, color, and pattern of feathers, but I look for combinations that enhance the underlying form rather than obfuscate it. This has led me to select simpler plumages and is why I opted for the simple gray of the male—to accentuate the shape and form of the flying bird and to reinforce the simplicity of the composition as a whole.

Points of attachment are a necessary part of sculpture. A bird in flight cannot stand alone: it needs some form of contact, some means of support to hold it aloft. The necessary connections are important structurally, but not visually. I try to make them as inconspicuous as possible. But trying to hide a connection can bring more attention to it rather than less. People start looking for the trick instead of looking at the piece. I avoid conspicuous tangencies that call attention to themselves. Connections that are overly fussy and delicate invite unwanted attention as well. Rather than trying to hide the connection, I try to design it in such a way that makes it immediately obvious, immediately understood, and then immediately ignored. I hide it in plain sight.

With my Marsh Hawk, the point of contact is obvious: a reed brushes alongside the bird's tail. The contact is simple and solid, easily understood and easy to move beyond. There is no reason to dwell. There is no mystery; no time need be spent wondering where, what, or how. The reed and the tail both continue on past the point of contact, carrying your eye away from it. The bird's wings and the all-important wingtips remain free and clear of any encumbrance.

The idea is to get beyond the connection and the issues of support as quickly as possible so that the attention goes instead to the object that is supported: a slender Marsh Hawk gliding gracefully over the reeds, rocking gently on angled wings, alternating from dark to light as it moves back and forth across the open space of the marsh.

I would rather create a piece that gains strength and becomes more and more interesting over time than a piece that makes a dramatic impression the first time you see it but never does so again.

END OF AUTUMN

Yellow-rumped Warbler & Goldenrod

Transitions

One of the reasons I enjoy living in southwestern Pennsylvania is that the area is blessed with four distinct seasons. They are not only cleanly and clearly defined, but also equally weighted. This suits me because I don't have a favorite season. I enjoy each one as it takes center stage, puts on a magnificent show, and then graciously gives way to the next. Each has its own merits and unique beauty. Over the years, I have come to realize it isn't the individual seasons that appeal to me as much as the transitions between them. While I fully embrace the perfect days we all associate with each season, I find the subtle clues indicating a season is on the way in or out are more interesting to me than the day-to-day sameness of any one season at its height.

If you aren't paying attention, if you look away, even for a day or two, there are times when seasonal transitions can seem abrupt and dramatic, like the seemingly "sudden" changes that amaze us in a fast-growing child we only see occasionally. But if you are observant and attentive, the transitions are more gradual, subtle, and revealing.

Sometimes the variations of a singular beauty followed through the seasons can provide a clearer sense of why I am drawn to a subject. And that, in turn, can determine the direction I want to take artistically. Goldenrod puts on a spectacular late-summer show. At its flowering height, it can be the dominant feature of an open landscape. Its very abundance affects how it is perceived. Visually, it registers as a collective whole rather than as single plants. An entire field in bloom reads as one giant mass. The extravagant display tempts me as a painter, but an expansive landscape is a difficult subject to sculpt.

Summer fades into autumn, which, in turn, gives way to winter. Lush growth falls away, exposing simpler and simpler lines. Wind and weather strip away the exuberance of a goldenrod field and expose the spare, elegant lines of bare stems. Etched against the white canvas of an early snow, the plants that still stand can now be seen as individuals. What was once an overwhelming chorus has been distilled into the single voice of a clean, pure line. I find the minimal simplicity of goldenrod late in the year to be just as beautiful as when the plants were in full bloom. And now, as a sculptor, I see an opportunity in the graceful elegance revealed by winter.

End of Autumn
36 x 12 x 12
acrylic on basswood,
brass, and bronze
2011

There are many different kinds of birds likely to be found in an overgrown field. I chose a Yellow-rumped Warbler for a number of reasons. Its small size enabled the goldenrod to maintain its role as an equal element in the composition. A larger bird would have become dominant and reduced the goldenrod's role and importance. Sparrows are similar in size to the warbler and even more likely to be found among the weeds, but they tend to have more bulk and heavier bills. I felt the delicate proportions of the slender-billed warbler would do a better job of reinforcing the feel of exquisite delicacy established by the goldenrod. A somewhat obscure reason to choose a Yellow-rumped Warbler is based on my knowledge of the bird's habits more than its physical appearance. In my area, Yellow-rumped Warblers are migrants rather than permanent residents. They pass through in large numbers during fall migration, an event that carries with it the bittersweet recognition that the year is winding down and winter is on the doorstep. It seemed fitting that a composition inspired to some degree by the change of the seasons should include a bird of passage. What better way to acknowledge the poignancy that comes with the year's end than to incorporate the symbolism inherent in a fall migrant?

It can be so easy to discount a weed as nothing more than just a weed. But the unexpected beauty that can be found in low and humble places is often the purest kind. Sometimes the more worthy effort lies not in capturing a magnificent spectacle, but in lifting up a small thing that is easily overlooked.

WINTER WAXWINGS

Cedar Waxwings & Pussy Willow

Restraint

A friend and I were talking one day about things in nature that we both found attractive. Waxwings and pussy willow came up in the conversation separately, but our talk brought them together in a way I had not previously considered. The combination was a good one and got me thinking harder about waxwings.

Black masks, crests, yellow tail bands, and bright red accents make waxwings one of the most striking and colorful songbirds. At the same time, they are one of the most subtle, with silky smooth gradations of incredibly soft and delicate hues. This dichotomy extends to their behavior. A flock of waxwings can be a noisy, animated gang of enthusiastic marauders that strip a tree of fruit in a matter of minutes. Or, especially in the colder months, they can perch quietly, remaining silent and still for long periods of time.

Pussy willow has a similar dual personality. It spends most of the year looking much like any other small tree, and then for a brief time it becomes most decidedly unlike other trees as its buds burst open like popcorn to form the long, white-tufted wands that are familiar to so many as a symbol of spring.

The more I thought about waxwings and pussy willow, the more I wanted to portray the quieter side of both the birds and the willow. The piece became an exercise in restraint. It became more about holding back rather than going for broke. It became more about what to leave out than what to put in.

While I was working on the design, I came across a line in a novel that made me stop and think. The novel was a legal thriller that dealt with all the trappings in a world of power and influence. The words that caught my eye were, "gold is cheap, quiet is expensive." The context in the story was a comparison of law offices. The pretentious office loaded with gleaming chrome and glass was designed to look impressive, but the quiet, subdued office that offered no flash was where the real power lay.

There were opportunities to jazz up the waxwing piece at every turn—to add more birds, more action, more flash. But the main idea I had settled on was a quiet one. I wanted to emphasize the quiet, subtle side of the willow and the birds. I had fallen in love with the sense of timelessness that went hand in hand with the peace, quiet, and stillness of waxwings in winter.

As I continued to make decisions about the composition, I resisted the constant temptation to "turn up the volume." *Winter Waxwings* remains a quiet piece. It's meant to be a piece that stays with you. It's one that grows on you over time rather than giving up all its secrets at the start.

Winter Waxwings
39 x 16 x 14
acrylic on tupelo
2013

I had admired both waxwings and the elegant wands of pussy willow, but had never thought of the two together. Once I made the connection between them, the combination seemed obvious.

Very quickly, this became a cold-weather piece. Waxwings are unusually smooth and silky. Other than wings and tails, their feathers have very little definition. Their plumage can appear more like fine hair than feathers. As the birds puff up their feathers in cold weather, their shapes become more interesting and more believable. The shape of a waxwing fluffed up against the cold of winter is far more sculptural to my eye than the sleek smooth shape of the same bird in summer. And likewise, the slender twigs of willow are more interesting with the definition provided by their swollen buds. I wanted to capture a specific time of year—late winter on the cusp of spring—still cold enough to chill the birds but warm enough to swell the buds of the willow.

This piece is not about the waxwings. It isn't about the pussy willow. The piece is about the relationship between the two. The real subject of *Winter Waxwings* is the peaceful stillness formed by the delicate balance that holds the birds and branches together. Creating and maintaining that balance was the goal, and the challenge, at every stage.

The finished piece is calm and serene, but I struggled more than usual to make it so. I considered including more birds in the composition. At one point I had as many as seven, but greater numbers made it more difficult to maintain the willow's role as an equal partner. A group of three was enough to establish the idea of a flock without any of the birds losing their importance as individuals. The sensitive balance in the piece required the birds and branches to be equally weighted. Proportions were critical. Any more, or less, of either bird or branch would tip the scales one way or the other.

A Sand County Almanac is a collection of essays masterfully written by the noted conservationist Aldo Leopold. In an essay entitled "Good Oak," Leopold expresses the idea of a burning log in his fireplace releasing the light and heat of all its days in the sun. Although Leopold's log released its energy quickly in the blaze of an evening fire, the idea of storing up energy and releasing it is something I think about quite often with my birds.

It pleases me to think of the energy that I put into my birds as being released to the viewer over time. Ideally, I would like whatever beauty that is contained in my work to be dispensed to the viewer slowly rather than used up in a first encounter. I want the piece to have the capacity to grow on the viewer over time rather than to start to fade after an initial viewing. The quieter a piece, the more likely that is to happen. Just like quiet moments in our lives, quiet pieces are inherently more conducive to the kind of reflection and introspection that can become more meaningful with the passage of time. Subtlety is a key to long-term success. I'd rather suggest and whisper than demand and shout. I'd like my work to have elements and features that wait patiently, until the viewer is ready, to reveal themselves. The gesture in a foot, the tilt of a head, one feather overlapping another, a well-placed split, a gall, the lime-green layer beneath the bark of a freshly snapped branch, the swell of the pussy willow buds announcing warmer weather is coming, the lofted plumage of the birds saying that it is still cold. None of these things is screaming for attention, but they are all there. The secondary and tertiary elements that gradually come to the fore, in the end, are what the piece is really about.

We humans often equate crowds with action. The bigger the crowd, the more we expect something to happen. We gather together for an event or a show because something is going to take place. Birds flock together for just the opposite reason. Finding safety in numbers, they gather together to rest, to loaf, and to do nothing. Rather than looking for action, they are trying to avoid it.

Winter Waxwings presents the quiet calm of a resting flock. What I have included is what I felt was necessary to convey that idea—nothing more and nothing less. But there is always a temptation to add more—to spice things up. I was tempted to add another bird—or two, or three, or even four. I could have opened a wing or spread a tail. It was tempting to make the birds brighter and more colorful. It would have been so easy to light up the fireworks that the pussy willow could have provided. Opening up the pussy willow buds could have been eye-catching, but it would have changed the piece entirely, shifting it from the stillness of winter to the exuberance of spring. I could look at each of these possibilities as an opportunity lost. Instead, I see each one as a temptation averted. Just because I could have included so much more doesn't mean that I should have. I resisted all of the possible additions because none of them would have furthered the main idea. Each would have taken the piece further away from what I had in mind.

The rich and complex variety of the natural world provides the inspiration for my work. My job is to distill what I have seen into a simpler sculptural form. Sometimes it is harder to decide what to leave out than what to include. The simplest version of the piece is often the strongest.

Winter Bohemians

Bohemian Waxwings & Sumac

"One's art goes as far and as deep as one's love goes." —Andrew Wyeth

I can't think of a better way to get to know a bird than to carve it. With every step of the process, I become more familiar with the birds that I love.

The first thing that is required is a proper introduction. For me, that means observations of the bird in the field. Ideally, a chance presents itself to observe the bird even more closely in hand. Sketches from these observations lead to clay studies. In clay, my knowledge of the bird takes on a new dimension, literally, as I move from two-dimensional sketches to three-dimensional maquettes. Working in clay, I concentrate on identifying the attributes that capture the essence of the bird—a unique attitude or gesture, a characteristic stance, or a nuance of behavior. And then I move on to wood, roughing out the basic shape and continuing on with progressively finer techniques, making modifications and adjustments that get me closer and closer to understanding and expressing the truth about that particular bird. My effort to describe the bird as completely as I can continues with the delineation of the plumage—not just down to individual feathers, but down to the texture of those feathers, down to every last feather barb.

When the carving is complete, I have had the pleasure of spending time with each and every feather and have resolved every square millimeter of the bird's entire surface. At that point, I go back and revisit every feather with paint. I use color and pattern, value, and hue to emphasize the shape and form and bring out the beauty of the feathers with which I have become so familiar.

One of the things I enjoy most about my work is that I am able to work in such a painstakingly thorough and exhaustive manner. I get to do whatever it takes to do the job right. I enjoy being able to give as much time, attention, and effort as I feel I must to every aspect and detail of the project at hand.

It always surprises me when someone notes the time-consuming nature of my work and comments on how much patience I must have. I do not think of myself as being overly patient. Perhaps I am, but the way I see it, patience is something that is required to get through something that you don't want to do. Since I enjoy what I do, patience isn't as much of an issue as many might think. Does it take patience to get through a good thick book? No. If you are caught up in a good story, you find yourself wishing it could go on longer rather than end too quickly. As eager as you are to find out how the story ends, you are sorry when it does. Each bird has a story to tell. The better the story, the longer I hope it will last. I am fortunate. What I want to do and what I must do to get it done are one and the same.

Winter Bohemians
26 x 12 x 12
acrylic on basswood
2014

Winter Bohemians followed closely after *Winter Waxwings. Bohemians* came about as a continuation of the waxwing theme and brought it to a logical conclusion.

Both species of waxwing appealed to me greatly. In fact, from the very beginning when I first decided to do waxwings and pussy willows, I had wondered whether I should be taking advantage of the colorful plumage of bohemians. The bohemians seemed bigger and better in every way. At one point, before I made a final decision on species, I painted one of my clay Cedar Waxwings as a bohemian. The exercise showed me just how different the two species really are. The Cedar Waxwing I had painted as a bohemian didn't look right at all, but the painting experiment did help me decide that Bohemian Waxwings didn't really belong in the pussy willow piece. The petite and delicate Cedar Waxwings were a much better fit for the slender, graceful twigs of pussy willow, especially in a piece that was relying so heavily on subtlety.

Bohemian Waxwings were bigger, brighter, and bolder than cedars, but they were going to have to wait a little longer.

While I worked on Cedar Waxwings and pussy willow, I continued to think about the bohemians and what would provide an ideal setting for them.

For years, I had wanted to use the strong shape and color of winter sumac heads in a composition. I had considered a number of different options but was still looking for the right bird to make it work.

Whenever I talked about the differences between Bohemian Waxwings and Cedar Waxwings, I used the word "robust" to describe the bohemians. "Robust" is the same word I had always used to describe sumac heads. Suddenly, the common denominator of a simple word provided me with the combination I had been looking for. This is the first time I have resolved a compositional issue with the help of an adjective. I can't think of a better word to describe both the birds and sumac.

Traits move back and forth between the two. Both have rich color, full-bodied forms, and touches of red and chestnut. The waxwings' crests match the graceful curves of the sumac tops the birds rest on.

In the field, I learned very quickly that a sumac head that looks great from a distance can be pretty rough up close. As I moved from patch to patch, each head seemed to look better than the last, and very soon I had filled the car. Sorting through the samples back in the studio, I realized some of the heads I had collected were far cleaner and more striking than the others. I had accidentally discovered Smooth Sumac, *Rhus glabra*. Smooth Sumac had deeper color and was longer, leaner, leggier, and, to my eye, more elegant in every way than the more familiar Staghorn Sumac. And true to its name, it was smooth, without the hairy covering that makes Staghorn Sumac so coarse and rank up close.

Smooth Sumac made the combination of bohemians and sumac even better. I could now add elegance to the list of shared traits. I went back to the field for more samples and found that the heads of Smooth Sumac grow with quite a bit of swing to the left or right rather than perfectly upright. I used their curvature to build some circular motion into the design of the piece, especially in the head down low.

As is so often the case with an elaborate and complex habitat, the sumac was far more time-consuming than the birds were. I had never made sumac before, so it was also the fun part. The sumac heads are made out of fine bronze rod that I've welded together with a small jeweler's torch.

It is not my goal to impress people with how difficult it is to make a piece. I don't want the viewer to be weighed down with the burden of its making. The struggle to bring a piece into being is my concern—the technical challenges fall to me. If I am successful, the viewer will be blissfully unaware of the effort that has been expended and simply bask in the beauty of the thing made.

CURVES AND ANGLES

Carolina Wren & Christmas Fern

Unexpected company

On more than one occasion, I've had a Carolina Wren come and join me in my studio. My shop is on the second floor. Years ago, a wren found a way into the garage below and made its way up the stairwell and into the studio. When most birds realize they're caught inside, they flail against the windows in a panic. But not wrens. Wrens are very comfortable in enclosed spaces. The family name for wrens is *Troglodytidae*, meaning "cave dwellers." The wren knew how it had gotten into my studio and it knew how to get out. I was working at the carving bench, but when the wren came up the stairs, I put my chisels down, sat back, and watched. It made its way around the entire studio, checking out all the nooks and crannies. It hopped from one piece of shop equipment to the next. It paused on the band saw and then dropped to the floor and bounded over to me, cocked its head to the side, and looked directly at me. I tried not to move, but the bird knew I was there. We enjoyed a few silent moments together, and then it moved on. It found its way back downstairs and was gone.

A few years later another wren stopped by for a visit. Maybe it was the same bird, maybe not. The second bird spent time among my old clay models. It flew from the back of a jaeger to a cobwebbed wingtip of the flying marsh hawk and then perched incongruously on the dusty head of the clay snowy owl.

More recently, as I was walking to the house I saw a wren ahead of me sitting on the floor of the front porch in the same spot where I often sit. I slowed my approach. The bird did not fly. I got quite close before I stopped altogether, and the bird continued to sit for a minute or two before departing. A week later, a wren appeared on the deck railing right outside my studio window. This time I suspect it was the same bird. It sat for a long time on the wide railing at eye level and only a few feet away. It was a welcome opportunity to admire the bird without the distraction of action or habitat.

The wren on my porch and deck reminded me of the simplicity of my *Green Heron*'s presentation. I enjoy the way freestanding pieces bring a heightened focus and attention to the bird. I am always on the lookout for a bird that lends itself to this format. My experiences with the wrens in and around my studio got me thinking that a Carolina Wren might be a good candidate for my next freestanding piece.

Curves and Angles
6 x 8 x 15
acrylic on basswood
2014

I had made a quick sketch of the wren on my porch. I used it along with the encounters I'd had with the wrens in and around my studio to make a clay model. The model matched the angles of the body, bill, and tail in the sketch, but it didn't look quite the same. The real birds had looked alert and animated even while resting quietly, but in my clay study the contact of the bird's belly with the ground made the bird look heavy and sluggish.

The discrepancy between the real bird and my clay model caused me to step back and reassess. What was it about the small bird that made it so appealing? Looking ahead to a finished piece, what aspect of the wren did I most want to capture and convey? Do the attributes of this lovely little bird have a common denominator? Can I reduce it to a single idea? Questions like these run through my mind while I am working out the design of a piece. I try to identify why I am doing the piece and what is important about it so that I have a basis for making decisions. Once I determine my reason for doing a piece, then each decision can be made in light of how it will further the main objective.

Carolina Wrens pack a huge amount of character into a tiny, energetic bundle. Their rich rusty color and bold white eye stripe combined with the strong angles of their curved bills and jaunty upturned tails give them an irresistible attitude and spirit. I wanted my carving to capture the bird's lively, vibrant disposition.

Top: Carolina Wren
drawn from life
pen and ink
5 x 7
Bottom: Carolina Wren
raised clay model
polymer clay
actual size

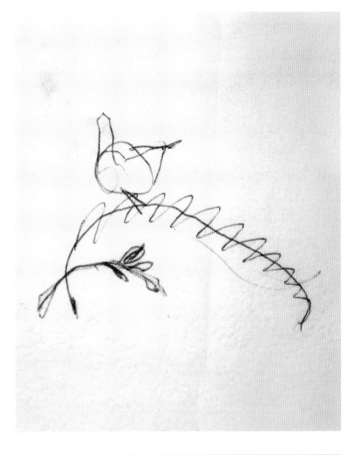

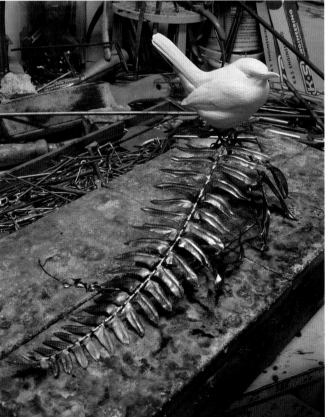

I started to realize once again that simply duplicating what I had seen would not be enough. I was going to have to raise my carved bird up off its belly to convey the attitude projected by the real bird. My bird needed more height. This small deviation, raising the bird up onto its legs, triggered changes that altered the piece significantly from what I had originally intended.

All my previous freestanding pieces had been larger birds with feet, wings, or tails that could touch down to help with support. I wasn't sure the smaller carved wren would be able to stand on its own. I needed a way to reinforce and support the wren's delicate feet and legs. I considered a small composition of twigs and dead leaves to provide the height and support I needed. It would have been entirely appropriate, given the birds' preference for low and tangled places. But I felt placing the brown bird in a brown setting would have made the bird blend in, and I wanted it to stand out.

Fern became the answer. Dark green ferns imply the shady recesses wrens favor and would provide the color contrast that would make the wren's rich rusty browns show up well. Ferns could easily give me the little bit of elevation I was looking for, while still keeping the piece low and simple.

Breaking away from my original idea made *Curves and Angles* more lively and more vivid, and made it a stronger piece of sculpture.

Top: Carolina Wren and fern
working conceptual drawing
ballpoint pen on napkin
6 x 6
Bottom: *Curves and Angles* in progress:
gessoed bird, ready-to-paint fabricated fern, and
welded and brazed copper, bronze, and steel

Working out a composition always involves looking for ways to tie elements together. I had introduced the fern as a means of getting some height into the piece. Initially, I had the arc of the fern much higher. Every time I lowered the arc, I liked it better. I continued to relax the arc incrementally and found that it looked best when it matched and repeated the same curves found in the wren's head and bill.

Christmas Fern is one of the simpler ferns that seemed appropriate for a simple piece. The simple shapes of its leaflets are not as lacy and busy as twice- and thrice-cut ferns that might rival the wren for attention. The rounded angular shape of the individual leaflets of the fern reminds me of the rounded angular shape of the wren. Each leaflet has an angular spur as it nears the stem, just like the cocked tail of the wren. The paired pattern of the simple leaflets echoes the barred pattern found in the wren's wings and tail.

I considered adding a second frond to reinforce the rhythm of the first, but found that the structure and geometry in one frond was enough. But I still needed a wider point of contact to keep the piece from falling over. I included an old frond, dead and dried, down low to provide the necessary third point of contact. Ironically, it's often the old growth added to a botanical subject that makes it look natural and alive. The parts that are dead or damaged can be more convincing than the parts that are green and growing.

The fern supports the plumage of the wren in two ways. The old dead frond reinforces the wren's coloration by repeating it, and the live green frond provides a contrasting backdrop that complements the wren's color and sets it off.

The old frond down low in the composition is like a bowstring connecting the two ends of the live fern arching above it. It holds the curved frond in tension, giving the piece a subtle bit of energy. The energy in a strung bow is not unlike the energy in the dynamic wren. Both are ready to go even when they are at rest.

The old frond starts and ends in the same places as the live green frond, but it swings wide to provide a point of contact far enough out to hold the piece up. In order to accommodate the beginning point and the end point along with a third wider point, I ended up making a sharp bend in its stem. I was surprised that

the kink seemed to work as well as it did among all the smooth, even curves, until I realized the angle of the stem's kink was the same angle as the wren's cocked tail. Both of the strong shapes in the wren were repeated in the strong shapes in the fern—the wren's bill in the upper frond, and the wren's tail in the lower one—bird and habitat working together.

The smaller green frond was added last. It had no part to play structurally, but I felt it was necessary compositionally. It brought the piece more fully into the round. Without it the composition seemed a bit linear and two-dimensional. The small frond balanced the long extension of fern heading out in the other direction and kept the wren in the visual center of the piece. It also adds just enough busyness and complexity to suggest the rest of the scene.

Every piece is the result of a series of intentional decisions, each of which is affected by the others. A few major decisions supported by countless smaller ones collectively build an integrated whole in which every element has a role to play and all the components are held in balance.

DRAWN TO WATER

A Series in Miniature

"If there is magic on this planet, it is contained in water." —Loren Eiseley

Water excites me. In many ways, it has been just as important to me as birds have been. For me, water is the primary feature of any landscape that includes it and I am drawn to it, just as I am drawn to birds. Once I arrive at the water's edge, I need to get out on the water in my canoe—to feel it, to become a part of it, to experience it more fully. I feel compelled to follow the magical line that forms where land and water meet. I never tire of exploring a shoreline.

Water is our most basic need, vital to our very existence. It is life itself, and yet in so many ways it remains a mystery. How can you describe water? How do you put into words what it looks like? It has an elusive, abstract alchemy that defies description. It is constantly changing right before our eyes. Sometimes it allows us to see right through it, and sometimes it reflects everything around it. Sometimes we see it directly, and other times we perceive it more clearly through its effect on the things that are in it, on it, and under it. I am fascinated with the ever-changing nature of water and how it moves back and forth between tangible and intangible. I have leaned over the side of a boat or dock and studied the water's surface in the same way I stare into the flames of a fire, lost in thought and wonder. I will spend my lifetime trying to know water better and learn its secrets.

The elusive and abstract nature of water does not lend itself very easily to a medium that is as literal as mine. I can make a rock or a leaf that looks just like a real rock or leaf, but how can I make water that looks just as real? The answer is, I can't. In my life-size pieces, where I present things the way they actually are, water does not show up very often, and when it does, it is more likely to have an implied presence rather than a literal one.

But not all my pieces are life-size. Working in miniature on the three pieces in this chapter opened the door to interpretation in a way that working in life-size could not. The simple fact that a piece is not actual size enables the viewer to more easily accept and see what I present as a *representation* rather than the real thing. Miniature scale breaks the spell that holds life-size work to a higher standard of realism. In miniature, I feel freer to portray water sculpturally by giving the viewer the *impression* of water rather than striving to duplicate it in a more rigidly literal way.

The pieces in my water series are very personal expressions of what I care most deeply about. To me, they represent far more than the birds that are included in them. Though they are small, I feel they are perhaps the most important pieces I have done.

Algonquin
4 x 14 x 9
acrylic on basswood and cherry
1982

193

A canoe is the best means of getting to the inaccessible places that I have always wanted to explore: the deepest, densest part of a marsh or swamp, the most remote and hidden pond, a winding river choked with rocks and drift-wood. As a teenager, I started heading north each summer on extended canoe trips deep into the interior of Algonquin Park in Ontario, Canada. Algonquin is a vast expanse of pristine canoe country. The park covers nearly 3,000 square miles of northern forest. The landscape is filled with countless lakes linked by a maze of rivers and portages. It is a land of wild bogs, rugged shores, twisting rivers, and hidden coves. The park is a paradise of windswept open water, black chutes sliding into foaming rapids, and quiet beaver ponds. For me, Algonquin Park is sacred ground. It has become my Eden, and I have returned to it every year to spend a week or two living outdoors, traveling by canoe, filling my cup with solitude, and restoring my soul.

The iconic symbol of Algonquin could easily be a moose, wolf, or beaver, but I have always identified a landscape with the birds that are a part of it, so I think of the loon as the best representative of the northern wilderness. Whether it is the loon's wild laughter or its mournful wail, the call of the loon captures the spirit of the north woods like no other sound.

McIntosh Lake
Algonquin

In 1982 I was carving full-time. I was busy with commissions and competitions. I was selling everything I made, but I was still looking for my first blue ribbon. It seemed all my energy was directed toward what I thought clients or judges were looking for. At a certain point, I needed to take a step back and do a piece for myself—to carve something that was important to me.

I decided to carve a pair of loons. Loons are large birds; a life-size pair would leave very little room to include much else. I wanted to include some context. I wanted *Algonquin* to represent not just loons, but also the landscape they are a part of. I wanted to convey the essence of the northern canoe country that had become so meaningful to me. When context and setting are as much a part of a piece as the birds, it's time to consider doing the piece as a miniature. *Algonquin* was about a place as much as it was about loons. It was my first miniature.

Algonquin was also my first piece to receive a blue ribbon in professional competition. I had never been able to win a blue ribbon in all the years I had tried to carve what I thought the judges were looking for. It wasn't until I quit carving for the judges, disregarded competition, and carved a piece for myself that I finally got the blue. It was a valuable lesson, and I have been carving what I have felt strongest about ever since.

I knew the loons would be carved out of wood, but I considered other materials for the water. I explored a number of options, such as two-part resins, plastics, and glass. These materials were waterlike, but none of them seemed to match up well with the inherent warmth of wood. Since they were transparent and clear, they duplicated many of the physical properties of water, but the nature of each seemed too different from that of wood to work compatibly with the carved birds.

In the end, I decided *Algonquin* would be a stronger piece of sculpture if I could find a way to artistically *represent* water rather than try to physically duplicate it. I chose to carve the water out of wood. I used cherry, a fine-grained hardwood, which I stained dark and burnished rather than painted. The stained wood had a depth of finish that introduced the idea of transparency in a way that opaque paint could not. The stain allowed the color of the cherry to show through enough to suggest the tea color that is often found in the tannin-rich water of northern lakes.

Algonquin was a pivotal piece for me. The subject matter was important to me personally, but of even greater significance was how the piece began to change my thinking and my approach to my work. With *Algonquin*, I became concerned less with carving techniques and detail and more with the larger sculptural issues of shape and form. The change can be understood in terms of lighting. *Algonquin* thrives on backlighting. In strong light, the surface detail falls away and the pure shape and form of the piece become more apparent and powerful. *Algonquin* looks best in light that would be considered too harsh and too directional for most of my pieces. Prior to *Algonquin*, I had thought of myself as a bird carver. It was while I worked on *Algonquin* that I started to think of myself as a sculptor who happens to carve birds.

I live beside the headwaters of Loyalhanna Creek. I'm two miles downstream from its source, the point where it wells up out of a wet field. The Loyalhanna is still a small stream as it passes by my house and studio. It's narrow and swift, falling fast from pool to pool. The Loyalhanna has been important to my life and my work, just as my beloved north woods canoe country has been. I spend one or two weeks each year up north, but I live, day in and day out, on the banks of the Loyalhanna.

The stream is a constant source of both inspiration and distraction. I see it every time I look up from my work. I hear the comforting rustle of water tripping over stones twenty-four hours a day. I built my studio to take advantage of my streamside view. Throughout the day, I watch the sunlight illuminating the pools in the morning and backlighting them into brilliance in late afternoon.

Every day I find an excuse to take a walk up or down stream. It's become a daily ritual to find a place to cross without getting my feet wet. Each day the Loyalhanna offers something new. If I give it my time and attention, it always has another lesson to teach me. The more time I spend with it, the better I know it, and the more important to me it becomes.

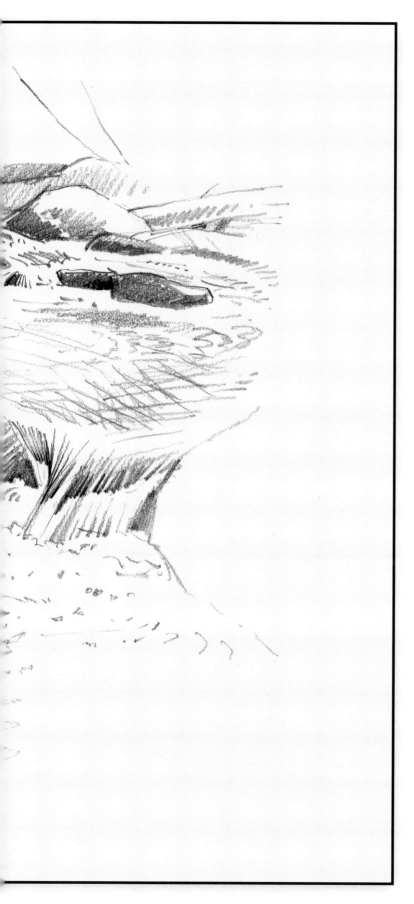

Water is a magnet to wildlife, and my stream is no exception. There is always something to see. I might look up just in time to see a mink disappearing into the rocks, a hen wood duck coaxing her new brood into the current for the first time, or a heron stalking in one of the deeper pools. Barred Owls watch for crayfish in the riffles. I find claws and exoskeletons on the railing of my studio deck in the morning and know the owls had a good night's hunt. The phoebes gather mud and moss from the rocks for their nests under the studio's eave. I have watched waxwings, tanagers, buntings, and a dozen other songbirds take their baths in the shallows. Mayfly hatches fill the air and spill into the studio if windows and doors are open. Louisiana Waterthrushes barrel up and down the corridor of the stream, pealing out a bold song that is always strong enough to be heard above the sound of rushing water.

Belted Kingfishers are regular visitors along my section of the Loyalhanna and are never shy about announcing their arrival. They sweep in with a rattling cry and take up an exposed perch with a good view of the stream. Kingfishers are handsome birds endowed with a generous dose of character. They always seem to be just as interested in the stream's trout as I am.

Loyalhanna Creek
Stahlstown, Pennsylvania
June 18

As with *Algonquin*, this is a piece that needed to be a miniature in order for the bird and the composition to be seen the way I intended. The kingfisher is part of the scene and gives it scale, but it is not the main subject. The kingfisher catches your attention, but the real subject of the piece is what has drawn the kingfisher's attention: Loyalhanna Creek.

The design of *Loyalhanna* centers on the eddy that is positioned like a bull's-eye in the center of the piece. The eddy is surrounded by concentric swirls of moving water that create the movement in the piece and hold your eye in the heart of the composition.

Eddies that form behind the obstacles in a moving stream or river are pockets of calm water that are especially useful to whitewater paddlers. They are safe havens where a paddler can hold a kayak or canoe and rest in the midst of a rushing stream. The eddy in *Loyalhanna* provides the same calm refuge where your eye can rest. From there, your eye moves out into the current, testing the water, but it returns, swept back again and again into the calm eddy. The weathered snag hung up on the rocks forms an angular spiral that takes your eye up and away from the water, but the placement of the kingfisher blocks that exit. The bird's gaze returns your eye to the eddy in the center of the piece. Its daggerlike bill points the way.

Loyalhanna
11 x 17 x 11
acrylic on basswood and walnut
1984

Loyalhanna is a smaller piece, but it required one of my biggest mockups. I went to the stream and built the situation with real rocks and logs, then waded out with a slab of clay on a board and tried to sculpt the moving water. The model helped me understand the basic shape and flow of the water around the rocks and log, but clay did not help me resolve the patterns on the water's surface. Clay was just as fluid as the water itself. It went wherever I pushed it. I wasn't able to resolve the surface of the water until I was carving with chisels in wood. The grain and structure of the wood provided the resistance I needed to bring a sense of order to the water's chaotic surface. I chose to carve the rushing water out of walnut. I had carved *Algonquin* with tighter grained cherry, but the livelier action of the water in *Loyalhanna* led me to select a wood with a more open grain pattern. Walnut's coarse grain added a more complex texture and a hint of shimmer to the surface that enhanced the impression of the rippled surface of moving water.

202

I don't usually have any difficulty letting my pieces go. In fact, the bigger they are, the easier it is for me to part with them. I suppose this is because the larger pieces are so time-consuming that by the time they are finally finished, I usually feel I have had more than enough time with them and I am ready and eager to move on. It is the smaller pieces that are harder for me to give up.

Loyalhanna has found a good home, but if I am ever asked if I have a favorite of all the pieces I have done, or if I could have one of my pieces back, *Loyalhanna* is the piece that comes to mind. This is another indication of how personal the water series pieces have been to me. They are more about the places that have been important in my life than they are about birds.

The Solitary Sandpipers I see in Pennsylvania are migrants passing through on their way north or south. The Solitary Sandpipers I see on our summer canoe trips in Algonquin Park are also migrants, already heading back down from their muskeg breeding grounds even farther to the north. In either place, solitaries are likely to be seen alone and found along the same tangled and secluded shorelines that also attract me.

We come upon them often while canoeing through the park. I am not surprised when one appears, because the setting usually alerts me to the possibility ahead of time. As we approach a shallow portage landing or paddle along a meandering beaver channel, I'll find myself thinking what a good spot this would be for a solitary, and a minute later the bird appears. There are certain spots where I have come to expect them.

I have sketched Solitary Sandpipers a number of times over the years. The accompanying sketch was drawn many years ago during our first canoe trip as a family. Eric was five, and Emily had just turned three. The trip was an exercise in paring life down to its simplest terms. We had food, shelter, and each other—everything we needed and nothing more. The four of us and all our possessions fit neatly in one 17-foot canoe. For an idyllic week we were alone, living deliberately, as Thoreau would say, while traveling through a landscape of unspeakable beauty.

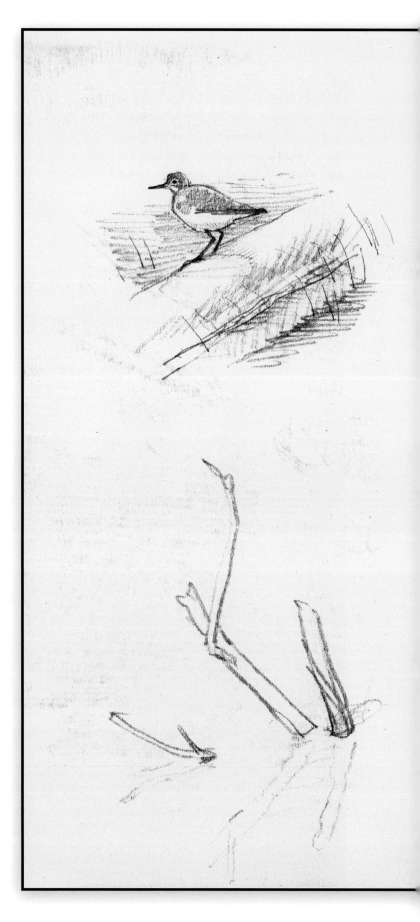

Solitary Sandpiper
Juan Lake, Algonquin Park
Ontario, Canada
July 28, 1991

204

205

Based on the original sketch, I envisioned a calm water surface, almost smooth, with just a few widening ripples. I knew from experience that carving such a subtle surface could be fussy and tedious. It is often easier to let the chisels bite into the wood rather than just nibble. Instead of trying to carve it subtly, my plan was to give the water much more action than I had intended and cut down the crests of the waves later to achieve the softer effect I was after.

But when I took a step back, I found my over-carved water wasn't as overly dramatic as I thought it would be. Rather than looking rough, it seemed to capture nothing more than a gentle, onshore breeze. So instead of letting the waves in deeper water flatten out as they moved into the shallows, I continued the rippling wave action all the way into the rocks.

Again, I was using stain rather than paint to darken the water. I kept the stain away from the areas where I wanted transparency to create the illusion of shallow water giving way to the dark-ness of deeper water and of the log sinking down into the depths.

When I first applied the stain, the wood did not take it evenly, and I was disappointed. But as I built up the depth of the finish with additional layers of stain, I was pleased to see a rock shelf appear and the irregular areas begin to suggest a subtle landscape of rocks underneath the water.

Solitude
7 x 25 x 16
acrylic on holly and walnut
2015

My deep ties to the canoe country that inspired this piece are only a part of what made this such a personal piece. The wood that I used for it had been given to me by my father. It was part of a pile he no longer had room for. At first the wide, thin walnut board seemed to have too many flaws to be of much use, but over time I began to realize that each of the board's imperfections could be aligned with the composition I had in mind. The wide swath of light sapwood along one edge was in just the right place to become the transparent shallows, the irregular burled grain in the area that would be close to "shore" could suggest underwater rocks, and the hollow pith that is so often a problem with walnut came out exactly where I wanted one of the sunken log's branches to come back up out of the depths. I didn't even have to drill a hole for the branch, and the growth rings in the walnut radiated out from it like expanding ripples. The board was perfect.

As I started to carve the water, I ran into a problem. My chisels are meant for carving birds. The selection of flat chisels, skews, and shallow gouges on my bench are ideally suited for carving the rounded, convex shapes of birds and feathers. *Solitude*'s water surface is composed entirely of concave hollows, which call for a different kind of carving and a different set of chisels.

Carving the troughs in the water required gouges with the right size, the right width, and the right sweep. I didn't have the gouges I needed, but I knew where to find them. My father is not a bird carver, but he is the one who got me started carving. He carves in a traditional European style and has a far more extensive selection of the deeper gouges I was missing. I could not have carved the water without the chisels I borrowed from my dad. It was especially meaningful to me that the wood for this piece came from my dad and I was able to carve it with the chisels he has used all of his life.

The three pieces in this chapter bracket the rest of the work in this book like bookends. *Algonquin* and *Loyalhanna* are the earliest pieces in the book, and *Solitude* is the most recent. The common theme of water ties the three together, and the water's increasing presence in each piece has driven the series forward. Working in miniature has allowed me to include more of the scene than I could have if working in full scale. As the series has developed, the emphasis has shifted from the birds to the setting. The overall dimensions of the pieces have increased while the birds themselves have gotten smaller. As the proportions have changed, the pieces have become more and more like small landscapes.

There was a time when I felt that "landscape" was subject matter beyond my reach as a sculptor. Initially, I saw the sandpiper sketch that led to *Solitude* as a more appropriate image for a painting than a carving because of the amount of landscape it included.

A few years ago, I began painting *plein air* landscapes. (It has been a longstanding goal of mine to return from my canoe trips with paintings rather than photographs.) It's only now that I am painting in two dimensions that I have been able to find a way to make the image I always thought of as a painting work as a piece of three-dimensional sculpture. *Solitude* might never have been completed in three dimensions if not for the work I am now doing in two dimensions.

Everything I do, everything I see, and everything I experience becomes a part of my work. New ideas are constantly being considered, adapted, modified, and integrated. The work continues to evolve, as it should.

ARTIST STATEMENT

Of all the exquisite designs I see in nature, I am most powerfully drawn to the shapes, colors, and patterns of birds. I simply marvel at their perfection. I will see something in the field that stirs my blood so deeply that I cannot help but respond artistically in an effort to better and more fully understand what I have seen. I want to hold onto that image as long as I can and somehow make it mine. Art is my way of taking possession of the beauty I see in the natural world. While I have always used art to further the relationship I enjoy with birds, I've come to realize that birds have been my means of exploring art, and art, in and of itself, is just as important to me as birds. Each has enhanced my understanding of the other, and in my work the two become one.

About the Author

1957   Born in Marinette, Wisconsin, to Donald and Alice Barth. His mother has a strong interest in nature, especially birds. His father is a civil engineer and an accomplished woodworker with a special interest in carving. Larry displays an early interest in the birds around the house built by his father on the shore of Lake Michigan's Green Bay.

1965   Moves to Bethel Park, a suburb of Pittsburgh, Pennsylvania, which provides a strong art education program as well as proximity to Carnegie Museum of Natural History and East coast carving shows.

1971   At the age of fourteen, carves his first bird—a miniature Rufous-sided Towhee. Also visits the bird banding operation at Powdermill Nature Reserve for the first time.

1972–74   Sells handfuls of tiny carved birds to a local florist for 25 cents apiece. Soon begins showing and selling his birds at weekend art fairs, which leads to representation in a local wildlife art gallery. Does pen and ink illustrations, including the cover art, for the revision of Joel Carl Welty's *The Life of Birds*, a college-level ornithological textbook. Begins volunteer work at Carnegie Museum's Section of Birds, cataloging study skins.

1975   Based on the fame of Cornell's Lab of Ornithology, applies to Cornell University and is accepted. A last-minute realization that his interest in birds is rooted in art rather than science causes him to switch to Carnegie Mellon University, where he enters the design program, heading toward a degree in illustration. Attends the Ward Foundation's Fall Exhibition during his freshman year and sees the work of other bird carvers for the first time.

1976   First attends the Ward Foundation World Championship Wildfowl Carving Competition held in Salisbury, Maryland. Enters the Novice Class with a miniature Great Blue Heron, which takes 3rd in Show.

1977	Returns to the Ward Show and enters the Professional Class with a miniature Red-tailed Hawk in flight, which takes 2nd in Show. The hawk sells for $4,500, a major sale that helps convince Larry that carving birds could actually be a way to make a living. Switches his major from illustration to "self-defined," which allows him to take any course in the college community that he feels can help him pursue his unique goals. He concentrates on design fundamentals, color theory, drawing, and anatomy.
1979	Enters his senior year thesis project, *Great Horned Owls*, in the Ward World Championship and places 2nd in World Class Decorative Life-size, the highest level of competition. One week later, he graduates with honors from CMU with a BFA in Design and begins carving full-time. Marries Linda and moves closer to Powdermill Nature Reserve's bird banding program.
1980	Participates for the first time in the Leigh Yawkey Woodson Art Museum's annual "Birds in Art" exhibition in Wausau, Wisconsin. His work has been included in the prestigious event every year since.
1985	Wins the World Class Decorative Life-size division at the Ward World Championship with *Winter Lakeshore*.
1986	Wins Best in World title with *Terns in Flight*.
1987–89	Travels to Alaska to study jaegers as part of the preliminary work for a major commission from the Leigh Yawkey Woodson Art Museum. Two years later finishes *Bering Sea Pirates*, his largest piece to date, in his new studio along Loyalhanna Creek near Stahlstown, Pennsylvania.
1991	Wins Best in World with *Vantage Point*. Later that year receives the Master Wildlife Artist medallion from the Leigh Yawkey Woodson Art Museum.
1992	Takes part in Artists for Nature (ANF) *Portrait of a Living Marsh* project in northeast Poland.
1993	Wins Best in World with *In the Cattails*.
1994	Takes part in ANF *Extremadura* project in central Spain.
1997	Wins Best in World with *Great Reed Warbler*, a piece inspired by his trip to Poland.
1999–2003	Wins title of Best in World for five consecutive years with *Green Heron, Tidal Companions, Broad-winged Hawk, Winter Sanderlings*, and *Red-billed Tropicbird*. In 2003 has first one-man show at Mass Audubon's Visual Arts Center (now the American Museum of Bird Art) in Canton, Massachusetts.
2005	Wins Best in World with *Indigo Buntings and Blackberry*.
2006	Travels to Hawaii to study 'I'iwis and wins Best in World with *'I'iwis and 'Ohi'a Lehua*.
2009	Wins Best in World with *Killdeer*.
2011	Wins Best in World with *End of Autumn*.
2013	Takes up *plein air* painting to fulfill a long-held desire to come away from annual wilderness canoe trips with paintings rather than photographs.
2014	Wins Best in World with *Curves and Angles*.
2015	Wins Best in World with *Winter Bohemians*.

LIST OF WORKS

Early Work

In the collection of the artist	In various private collections	
Rufous-sided Towhee	*Great Horned Owl*	*Sandpiper Pairs*
Black-throated Green Warbler	*Preening Yellowlegs*	*Carolina Wrens*
Yellow-shafted Flicker	*Screech Owl*	*Downy Woodpecker*
Great Blue Heron Pair	*Yellow-shafted Flicker*	*Goldfinch*
Red-tailed Hawk	*Cardinal*	*Robin*
Pileated Woodpecker	*Knot*	*Blue Jay*
Wood Duck	*Bobwhite*	*Song Sparrow*
White-breasted Nuthatch	*Ruffed Grouse*	*Meadowlark*
Ruffed Grouse	*Single Sandpipers*	*Chickadee*
		Barred Owl

Later Work

Great Blue Heron	*Ring-necked Pheasant*	*Carolina Wren*
acrylic on basswood	acrylic on basswood	acrylic on basswood
1976	1978	1980
Lost to fire	Private Collection	Private Collection
Red-tailed Hawk	*Great Horned Owl Family*	*Ruffed Grouse*
acrylic on basswood	acrylic on basswood and balsa	acrylic on basswood
1977	1979	1980
Private Collection	Collection of Audubon Society of Western Pennsylvania	The Miller Collection

216

Morning Serenade
Meadowlark and Pheasant
acrylic on basswood
1981
Private Collection

Fox Sparrow
acrylic on basswood
1982
Collection of Linda Barth

Wood Thrush
acrylic on basswood
1982
Private Collection

Algonquin
Common Loons
acrylic on basswood and cherry
1982
Collection of the artist

Algonquin
acrylic on basswood and cherry
1983
The Garfinkle Family Collection,
Ward Museum of Wildfowl Art,
Salisbury University

Screech Owl
Screech Owl and Polyphemus
Moth
acrylic on basswood
1983
Ella Sharp Museum

Eastern Kingbird
acrylic on basswood
1983
Ella Sharp Museum

*American Woodcock and
Cinnamon Fern*
acrylic on basswood
1983
Ella Sharp Museum

Northern Oriole and Cherry
acrylic on basswood
1983
Ella Sharp Museum

Silent Flight
Screech Owl and Luna Moth
acrylic on basswood
1984
Ella Sharp Museum

*Black-capped Chickadees and
Winterberry*
acrylic on basswood
1984
Collection of Tony and Louise
Foster

Broad-winged Hawk Bust
acrylic on basswood
1984
Ella Sharp Museum

Loyalhanna
Belted Kingfisher
acrylic on basswood and walnut
1984
Mass Audubon Art Collection,
Museum of American Bird Art

Winter Lakeshore
Snowy Owl and Bonaparte's Gull
acrylic on basswood
1985
Ward Museum of Wildfowl Art,
Salisbury University

Common Goldeneyes
acrylic on basswood and cherry
1985
Private Collection

American Kestrel
acrylic on polymer clay
1986
Collection of Margaret Webb

In the Tamaracks
Black-throated Green Warbler and
Black-and-white Warbler
acrylic on basswood
1986
The Garfinkle Family Collection,
Ward Museum of Wildfowl Art,
Salisbury University

Terns in Flight
Common Terns
acrylic on basswood
1986
Ward Museum of Wildfowl Art,
Salisbury University

In the Sycamores
Parula Warbler and Yellow-
throated Warbler
acrylic on basswood
1987
Ward Museum of Wildfowl Art,
Salisbury University

White-throated Sparrow
acrylic on basswood
1987
Collection of Shirley Soliman

In the Hemlocks
Blackburnian Warblers
acrylic on basswood
1987
Mass Audubon Art Collection,
Museum of American Bird Art

Baltimore Oriole
acrylic on basswood
1987
Collection of Jim and Patty
Sprankle

Bering Sea Pirates
Parasitic Jaegers and Arctic Tern
acrylic on basswood, tupelo, and
soapstone
1989
Collection of Leigh Yawkey
Woodson Art Museum

Scarlet Tanager
acrylic on basswood
1989
Collection of Jim and Patty
Sprankle

Ruby-crowned Kinglet
acrylic on polymer clay
1989
Collection of Tim TerMeer

Screech Owls Studies
acrylic on polymer clay
1990
Collection of Lars Jonsson

In the Pines
Northern Saw-whet Owl
acrylic on tupelo
1990
Collection of Sandor and Lorraine
Garfinkle

Red-billed Tropicbird
acrylic on basswood and soapstone
1990
Private Collection

Vantage Point
Loggerhead Shrike and Hawthorn
acrylic on basswood
1991
Ward Museum of Wildfowl Art,
Salisbury University

Spotted Sandpiper
acrylic on basswood
1991
Collection of Jay and Barbara Brost

Kestrel
acrylic on polymer clay
1991
Collection of Birgit and Robert
Bateman

Quiet Strength
Common Egrets
acrylic on polymer clay
1991
Collection of Peninsula Regional
Medical Center

Forbesway Drummer
Ruffed Grouse
acrylic on basswood
1992
Carnegie Museum of Natural
History at Powdermill

Waniewo Jackdaw
acrylic on polymer clay
1992
Collection of the artist

Whinchat
acrylic on polymer clay
1992
Collection of the artist

Red-necked Nightjar
acrylic on polymer clay
1992
Collection of the artist

Aquatic Warbler
acrylic on polymer clay
1992
Collection of Ysbrand Brouwers

Black-tailed Godwit
acrylic on polymer clay
1992
Collection of the artist

Blue-headed Wagtail
acrylic on polymer clay
1992
Mass Audubon Art Collection,
Museum of American Bird Art

Virginia Rail
acrylic on polymer clay
1992
Collection of Linda Barth

Screech Owl
bronze
Edition of 48
1992

Spotted Sandpiper
acrylic on basswood
1993
Collection of Masahiro Shimizu

In the Cattails
Least Bittern and Marsh Wren
acrylic on basswood
1993
Ward Museum of Wildfowl Art,
Salisbury University

Red-bellied Woodpecker
acrylic on basswood and tupelo
1993
Private Collection

Bluebird and Milkweed
acrylic on polymer clay
1993
Collection of Jeff and Donna
Leonhardt

Ruby-crowned Kinglet
acrylic on polymer clay
1993
Ella Sharp Museum

Snowy Owl
acrylic on polymer clay
1993
Collection of the artist

Golden-winged Warbler
acrylic on polymer clay
1993
Collection of Walter Matia

Mallard
pewter
1993
Ducks Unlimited, Loyalhanna
Chapter

In the Hardwoods
Pileated Woodpecker
acrylic on tupelo
1994
The Lamenza Family Collection

Lesser Kestrels
acrylic on polymer clay
1994
Collection of the artist

Little Owl
acrylic on polymer clay
1994
Artists for Nature Foundation

Bee-eaters
acrylic on polymer clay
1994
Collection of the artist

Short-toed Treecreeper
acrylic on polymer clay
1994
Collection of the artist

Indigo Bunting
acrylic on basswood
1994
Collection of Zachary L. Moyer

Pied-billed Grebe Pair
bronze
Edition of 48
1994

Pintail
pewter
1994
Ducks Unlimited, Loyalhanna
Chapter

Eastern Bluebirds & Milkweed
acrylic on basswood
1995
Collection of Roger W. Jones

Osprey & Atlantic Salmon
acrylic on basswood and walnut
1995
Private Collection

Carolina Wren
acrylic on polymer clay
1995
Collection of Katie and Donal
O'Brien

Prothonotary Warbler
acrylic on basswood
1995
Collection of Marian Rea Haight

Family Rhythms
Pileated Woodpecker family
acrylic on basswood and tupelo
1996
Collection of Gary and Barbara
Grendys

Bluebirds and Apple Blossoms
acrylic on polymer clay
1996
Collection of Katie and Donal
O'Brien

Great Reed Warbler
acrylic on basswood
1997
Ward Museum of Wildfowl Art,
Salisbury University

Song Sparrow
acrylic on polymer clay
1997
Collection of Willis and Donna
Buehl

Peregrine Falcon
acrylic on basswood and tupelo
1998
Collection of Roger W. Jones

Eastern Bluebird
acrylic on basswood
1998
Private Collection

Green Heron
acrylic on tupelo
1999
Ward Museum of Wildfowl Art,
Salisbury University

Eastern Phoebes
acrylic on basswood and tupelo
1999
Collection of the artist

Black-and-white Warbler
acrylic on polymer clay
1999
Collection of Tim TerMeer

Cerulean Warbler
acrylic on polymer clay
1999
Private Collection

Tidal Companions
Ruddy Turnstone and Purple
Sandpipers
acrylic on tupelo
2000
Ward Museum of Wildfowl Art,
Salisbury University

Cerulean Warbler
acrylic on basswood
2000
Collection of Zachary L. Moyer

Screech Owl
acrylic on polymer clay
2000
Collection of Masahiro Shimizu

Young Robin
acrylic on polymer clay
2000
Collection of Richard and Patsy
Buehl

Scarlet Tanager
acrylic on basswood
2000
Private Collection

Broad-winged Hawk
acrylic on basswood and tupelo
2001
Ward Museum of Wildfowl Art,
Salisbury University

Louisiana Waterthrush
acrylic on basswood
2001
Mass Audubon Art Collection,
Museum of American Bird Art

Ruby-throated Hummingbird
acrylic on polymer clay
2002
Collection of Herb and Helen
Buehl

Winter Sanderlings
acrylic on tupelo
2002
Ward Museum of Wildfowl Art,
Salisbury University

Eastern Bluebird
acrylic on basswood
2002
Collection of Anthony P. Picadio

Red-billed Tropicbird
acrylic on basswood
2003
Ward Museum of Wildfowl Art,
Salisbury University

Indigo Buntings and Blackberry
acrylic on basswood
2004
Private Collection

Black-capped Chickadees
acrylic on polymer clay
2005
Private Collection

'I'iwis and 'Ohi'a Lehua
acrylic on basswood
2006
Collection of Gary and Barbara
Grendys

Sanctuary
Hermit Thrush
acrylic on basswood
2007
Collection of the artist

Wind River Harmony
Mountain Bluebirds and Juniper
acrylic on basswood
2008
Private Collection

Killdeer
acrylic on basswood and maple
2009
Collection of Kirk and Nellie
Williams

Marsh Hawk
acrylic on basswood and tupelo
2010
Collection of Kirk and Nellie
Williams

End of Autumn
Yellow-rumped Warbler and
Goldenrod
acrylic on basswood
2011
Collection of Kirk and Nellie
Williams

Yellow-billed Cuckoo
acrylic on tupelo
2011
Collection of Kirk and Nellie
Williams

Winter Waxwings
Cedar Waxwings and Pussy Willow
acrylic on tupelo
2013
Collection of Kirk and Nellie
Williams

Curves and Angles
Carolina Wren and Christmas Fern
acrylic on basswood
2014
Collection of Kirk and Nellie
Williams

Winter Bohemians
Bohemian Waxwings and Sumac
acrylic on basswood
2014
Collection of Kirk and Nellie
Williams

Solitude
Solitary Sandpiper
acrylic on holly and basswood
2015
Collection of the artist